Inner Development

INNER DEVELOPMENT

SEVEN LECTURES

ROTTERDAM • 15-22 AUGUST 1938

by

VALENTIN TOMBERG

Translation revised by Richard and Patricia Bloedon

Anthroposophic Press

The original edition of this work was prepared with the consent of
Martin Kriele on behalf of the author and published by
Candeur Manuscripts in 1983.

Inner Development is translated from a German manuscript text
entitled *Sieben Vortrage über die Innere Entwickelung des Menschen.*

Published by Anthroposophic Press, RR4,
Box 94 A-1, Hudson, New York 12534.

Library of Congress Cataloging-in-Publication Data

Tomberg, Valentin.
   [Sieben Vorträge über die innere Entwickelung des Menschen. English]
   Inner development:seven lectures : Rotterdam, 15-22 August, 1938 /
by Valentin Tomberg ; translation revised by Richard and Patricia Bloedon.
   Translation of : Sieben Vorträge über die innere Entwickelung des
Menschen.
   ISBN 0-88010-363-9 (pbk.)
   1. Anthroposophy. I. Title.
BP595.T86 1992   92-13323
299".935—dc20   CIP

10 9 8 7 6 5 4 3 2 1

CONTENTS

Valentin Tomberg

$\mathcal{V}$alentin Tomberg, a controversial figure in the history of anthroposophy, was born on February 27, 1900, in St. Petersburg. The second son of a high government official, Tomberg grew up in Russia, in a Protestant (Evangelical) household, speaking Russian as his mother tongue. He had attended the Humanistic Faculty for only three semesters, studying history and philosophy, when his life—like that of so many others—was transformed by the Bolshevik Revolution of 1917, during which his mother was shot.

Before this, in Moscow, in 1915, Tomberg had already come into contact with the Theosophical Society. Russia was then enjoying a vital confluence of religious, spiritual, and occult streams. Consequently Tomberg, from an early age, was exposed to an entire range of possible spiritual paths, including of course the indigenous ones such as the Orthodox Church and The Old Believers. But it was the work of Rudolf Steiner that made the greatest impression upon him. By 1917, he was assiduously practicing the various exercises taught by Steiner in books such as *Knowledge of Higher Worlds and its Attainment, Theosophy, Occult Science—an Outline* and *A Road to Self Knowledge*.

Sometime in 1919-1920, while he was still in St. Petersburg, Tomberg encountered and worked together with members of a Hermetic, Rosicrucian group that had studied esotericism, including the Marseilles Tarot, under Gregor Ottonovich Mebes, Professor of Mathematics at Pages College. This group had gone underground after the Revolution, but the members whom Tomberg met were able to transmit to him much of what they had learned.

However, Tomberg did not stay long in St. Petersburg. By the middle of 1920 he was living with his father and elder brother, in Tallin (Reval), Estonia. He was never to return to Russia. In July, he wrote to Rudolf Steiner from Estonia:

Honored Doctor!

Three years ago I joined the Russian Theosophical Society and thereby made "spiritual culture" my goal. However, I could work neither with theosophical one-sidedness nor—above all—with Theosophy's customary unrestrained suppression of every free movement of thinking. On the other hand, your writings (*Knowledge of Higher Worlds, Occult Science, Theosophy, A Road to Self Knowledge* and others) showed that, besides the Theosophical there exists another movement in which precisely what I miss in Theosophy is to be found—namely, consideration for the reasoning faculty and for the uniqueness of each individual.

For this reason I turned to Anthroposophy. However, the reason I turn to you now, with the request to be taken into the circle of your students—for it is with that alone that this letter is concerned—is that, since 1917, I have practiced the meditation exercises given by you in your writings and results have been forthcoming. This last circumstance convinces me that it [Anthroposophy] is not charlatanry—that you really know what you are talking about, and also that the area I seek to enter is a dangerous one.

I do not wish to have the fate of that young mountain cow—of which the Buddha speaks—who, in search of new meadows and pastures, wandered into an unknown mountain range and fell into an abyss.

These two circumstances—trust in you and the seriousness of what I intend to undertake—are what prompt me to turn to you, Herr Doctor.

Respectfully,
Valentin Tomberg

In Tallin, Tomberg earned a living in various ways, while studying comparative religion and ancient and modern languages at Tartu University. In 1924, he became an employee of the Estonian Postal Service, which relieved him of financial worries and allowed him to dedicate himself to inner work. On July 4, 1924, he wrote another letter to Rudolf Steiner:

Most Honored Doctor!

With this letter I address myself to you to request admittance into the School of Spiritual Science in Dornach.

In the first place, I must inform you that I am not a member of the Anthroposophical Society, although I know several members, some of whom are friends of mine.

My esoteric strivings began in 1915. Since 1920 I have worked actively for the advancement of the anthroposophical *work*. This I understand to be essentially the dedicated activity that has as its goal the deepening of human consciousness by means of independent, dogma-free, authority-free, selfless, creative cognitive work, combined with the practice of self-criticism. I have for a long time striven to work in this way with friends in two small, closed circles.

What prompts me to write to you is not to seek "connection" with a human group, or to seek help, or relief (though it is certainly nice to pass responsibility onto others), but the conviction that I have a life-task that, as far as I presently know, can only consist in being useful in my own way to the *work* that Dornach should serve. Therefore I have decided to take on a difficult task that claims all my powers. I do *not* wish to enter a "spiritual boarding school" in which spiritual food is served ready-made. The Spiritual-Truth, the Spiritual-Validity, that I hope to find, I will learn to bring to realization along with the duties that follow from it—in order then to bear these as seeds into the future. I perceive what is coming as something difficult—therefore I will gratefully accept your decision, whatever it may be, with regard to my fate.

I am twenty-four years old. I have no profession, for as yet there is none for me. I dedicate my available powers and time to spiritual science and what it directly demands.

I have done many different kinds of work in life—clerk, teacher, agricultural worker, pharmacist, artist. I am poor and therefore cannot come to Dornach.

Awaiting your decision I remain—and will remain in the future—your grateful and humble co-worker in the work of realizing humanity's vocation and destiny—whether it is recognized or not....

Valentin Tomberg

In the following year, 1925, Rudolf Steiner died. Tomberg never met him personally. However he joined the Anthroposophical Society in Estonia, and became part of the small group of anthroposophists led by Otto Sepp—we find him giving lectures at the Danzig Members Conference in 1926 and 1927. At about the same time, he began to work intensively with the Foundation Stone Meditation that Rudolf

Steiner had given at the refounding of the Anthroposophical
Society at the Christmas Conference of 1923/24.

During the late 1920's Tomberg travelled in Germany and
Switzerland. Among others, he met Marie Steiner in Dor-
nach and Kurt Piper and Emil Leinhas, the editors of *Anthro-
posophie*, in Stuttgart, who asked him to contribute to their
"Weekly Journal for the Free Spirit" in which, between
March 2, 1930 and December 31, 1931, thirty articles
appeared. (These have been collected in *Early Articles*, Can-
deur Manuscripts, 1984). In the same year an article, "The
Philosophy of Taking Counsel with Others," appeared in *Das
Goetheanum* (September 28, 1930, collected in *Group Work*,
Candeur Manuscripts, 1985).

In 1932, Otto Sepp died and Tomberg became General Sec-
retary of the Anthroposophical Society in Estonia, under
whose auspices he began giving lectures—amongst others, a
series of sixteen lectures on the Apocalypse of St. John. With
these lectures, Tomberg found himself at the center of controversy, for certain members began to complain to Marie
Steiner that he was setting himself up as an independent spiritual authority. Tomberg, for his part, though he certainly
spoke out of his own experience and on the basis of his own
independent spiritual research, never maintained that he
taught or spoke anything other than anthroposophy or
worked in any other spirit than that of Rudolf Steiner. Many
of those around him recognized this and, indeed, requested
that he begin to write down the results of his spiritual
research. And so, beginning in Fall 1933, Tomberg began publishing his twelve *Anthroposophical Studies of the Old Testament*
(Candeur Manuscripts, 1985) in mimeograph form. During
this period, too, Tomberg married Marie Demski, who had
escaped from a Bolshevik labor camp thanks to a Russian
friend, Nikolai Belozwetov, who had married her in order to
enable her to flee with him to the West. This marriage was

subsequently dissolved and Marie Demski then married Tomberg. A child, Alexis, was born in 1933.

In the Introduction to his Old Testament Studies, Tomberg wrote:

The task of these publications, which are to appear regularly, is to meet the need existing among wide circles within the Anthroposophical Society for purely anthroposophical research. The content of the *Studies* has come about neither by the method of speculation based on reasoning and the setting up of hypotheses, nor by the mere summarizing of factual material contained in the lecture cycles of Rudolf Steiner—but by means of anthroposophical research.

The author is not in a position to mention all the cycles, books, and single lectures of Rudolf Steiner with which he has worked in order to come to the results presented in these studies; it will suffice to say, once and for all, that the author is indebted to Rudolf Steiner for all that has come to him in the way of knowledge. Everything which he has to say has its roots in the life work of Rudolf Steiner, so that he was also led to new sources of knowledge upon which he could then draw. As it is difficult to separate the air which one has breathed in from that of the outside world, so it is difficult for the author to draw a dividing line between the results of his own endeavor and that which Rudolf Steiner communicated.

These studies of the Old Testament were followed, beginning in 1935, by *Anthroposophical Studies of the New Testament*. In the Introduction to this work, besides acknowledging the primacy of Rudolf Steiner, Tomberg pays homage to "the work of anthroposophical friends on the New Testament." "In particular" he writes, "the works of Emil Bock, Dr. H. Beckh, and Dr. F. Rittelmeyer present collectively so useful and comprehensive a contribution to the deeper understanding of the Gospels that the author constrained to ask himself whether any extensive new work on the subject is necessary." He concludes with the hope that his work will "stir its readers to an interest in the writings of the circle of friends who lead the Christian Community."

Meanwhile, the controversy surrounding Tomberg grew more intense. Some felt that he was placing himself before Rudolf Steiner. Compounding this situation and fueling resentment was the fact that many of those close to Tomberg (such as Nikolai Belozwetov) thought most highly of him. In addition, rumors circulated concerning his marriage. Tomberg had written in the first of his studies about "eugenic occultism" and gossip now circulated that he, together with a small group, was intent upon founding the "sixth race." We find evidence of this suspicion in the correspondence of Marie Steiner. There is a letter of hers dated March 25, 1936 to an Estonian member, Miss von Dumpff, who had evidently been anxious about Tomberg's actions. At issue is whether Tomberg should continue as a First Class Member. As such, Tomberg is committed to represent anthroposophy to the world and not to present his own initiative without clearing it first with the Vorstand (Council) in Dornach. Is Tomberg promulgating another esotericism? Has Fräulein von Dumpff been "excluded" from the First Class? Have Tomberg and Belozwetov set themselves up as independent authorities? Are they practicing "eugenic occultism"?

Another, undated letter of 1936 makes clear what is at issue. Marie Steiner writes:

> We have been urgently requested to speak out plainly and without reservation about a situation in

which we wanted to exercise as much restraint as possible, because we do not wish to give up hope that a talented and formerly trusted member may find himself again after having fallen prey to youthful confusions. We are being asked questions that make it possible for us to sum up succinctly the matter which causes us so much pain. In so doing only a general outline of the problem becomes visible.

1. Is it permissible that material that is circulated, such as the Studies on the Old Testament by Mr. Tomberg, should carry the subtitle "anthroposophical studies"?

2. Is not the publishing of such material contrary to the will of the Dornach Vorstand, contrary to the express will of Dr. Steiner, who in an issue of the letters to the members indicated his wish that the permission of the Vorstand be obtained for anthroposophical activities (which would include such "anthroposophical studies").

To be sure, it is not permissible. In fact, Dr. Steiner made it clear to the active members' circle that permission of the Vorstand at the Goetheanum must be obtained for anything that occurs in the name of the Society. And it is especially a commitment that every First Class member takes upon himself as a member of the School of Michael not to pursue any other form of esotericism than that presented here.... Mr. Tomberg's behavior has radically transgressed the above conditions. Suddenly, and quite unexpectedly, he has presented himself to us in his "anthroposophical studies" as a new spiritual investigator. He has presented us with a *fait accompli*. To dismiss in advance any objections that might be raised, he has made rather reckless and arbitrary assertions in his first study and has mocked those who would not acknowledge other initiates.

3. Is it conceivable that a young man like Mr. Tomberg, who has just turned thirty-five years of age, already has the necessary maturity to be an occult teacher?...

Despite this controversy, however, Tomberg continued his work. In November, 1936, he issued the first of his *Studies on the Foundation Stone*, which was the fruit of eleven years of working with the Foundation Stone Meditation, and the first work to appear on the subject. Meanwhile, his work was becoming more widely known. Elizabeth Vreede, a member of the original Vorstand, having visited Tomberg in Estonia, recognized something of importance in his work, and was led to write the Foreword to the English edition of *Anthroposophical Studies in the Old Testament*. It was she who arranged for Tomberg to be invited to England and Holland to lecture.

In England, Tomberg was respected. George Adams, who wrote the introduction to the English edition of the *Studies on the Foundation Stone*, introducing the 1937 Summer School at Swanick, wrote of Tomberg as the author of "some of the most remarkable works which the Movement has produced in recent years." "It will be a privilege," he continued, "to welcome among so many other guests both old and new, one who comes from the North-Eastern countries of whose significance to the spiritual future Rudolf Steiner has told so much; one who will also be able to acquaint us with the present possibilities of the new spiritual life in those more distant lands." At Swanick, Tomberg lectured on the initiatory trials of fire, water, and air.

The next year, 1938, Tomberg again came to Britain, to the Summer School in Bangor, Wales. His topic was the work of the spiritual hierarchies in the twentieth century. Among nearly two hundred others, Elizabeth Vreede, Willi Sucher, and Ernst Lehrs were present. Following this meeting, Tomberg went to Holland where he gave the lectures on inner development presented here. At the urging of the friends he had made in Holland, and on account of the worsening situation in Estonia, Tomberg decided to move with his family to Holland.

In January of 1938 an article on "The Meaning and Significance of a Free Anthroposophical Group" appeared in the Dutch magazine, *Reports of Anthroposophical Endeavors* (see *Group Work*, Candeur Manuscripts, 1985). In Rotterdam during August of the year 1939, Tomberg gave the lectures published as *The Four Sacrifices of Christ*. Also in 1939 he began publishing the mimeograph copies that make up the (unfinished) *Studies in the Apocalypse*. But controversy continued to surround him.

Some time before the German invasion of Holland (May 10, 1940) Tomberg had a conversation with F. W. Zeylmans van Emmichoven, who had been appointed by Rudolf Steiner to be the head of the Anthroposophical Society in Holland. As a result of this conversation, Valentin Tomberg felt obliged to leave the Anthroposophical Society.

Tomberg continued to live and work in Holland, eking out a living by giving private language lessons. He moved to Amsterdam, where, conscious of the spiritual dimension of the war raging over Europe, he worked esoterically with the Lord's Prayer with one small group, while with another he worked with esoteric material given by Rudolf Steiner in the School for Spiritual Science. All this came abruptly to an end in the Spring of 1943.

Concerned for the Tomberg's safety, Ernst von Hippel, Professor of Law at Cologne University, who had come to know Tomberg through the Studies on the Old Testament, had thought they would be safer in Germany. As a respected law professor, von Hippel had sufficient influence to bring the Tombergs—who since the annexation of Estonia had become displaced persons—into Germany.

Around this time, certainly before the end of the war, perhaps while he was still in Holland—and according to one account, in a camp for displaced persons—Tomberg experienced a decisive call, as a result of which he converted to Roman Catholicism. Prior to joining the Roman Catholic Church, Tomberg had sought to pursue his path of anthroposophy first in the Christian Community and then in the Russian Orthodox Church, but he had found both these doors closed to him.

In Cologne, under the supervision of his friend, Ernst von Hippel, Tomberg began work on a Ph.D. Two small works of jurisprudence were published: in 1946, his Ph.D. thesis *Degeneration und Regeneration der Rechtswissenschaft* ("The Degeneration and Regeneration of Jurisprudence") and, in 1947, *Die Grundlage des Völkerrechts als Menschheitsrecht* ("International Law as Humanity's Right: A Foundation").

In 1948 the Tombergs moved to England—first to London, then to Caversham, near Reading. Tomberg worked there for the Foreign Service of the BBC, monitoring Soviet broadcasts. After initially attending some anthroposophical meetings, Tomberg lived from this time on, quietly and in seclusion, as a practicing Roman Catholic. He wrote two more works: one, published anonymously and posthumously, and written in French, called *Meditations on the Tarot: A Journey into Christian Hermeticism* (Element Books 1991) and the other, consisting of three small works ("The Miracle of the Awakening of Lazarus," "The Ten Commandments," "The Kingdoms of Nature, Humanity, and God") which, together with a fragment ("The Breath of Life"), are contained in *Lazarus komm heraus* (*Covenant of the Heart: Meditations of a Christian Hermeticist on the Mysteries of Tradition*, Element Books, forthcoming).

Valentin Tomberg died in 1973. Since then, his life and work have become the focus of controversy, mystification, and politicization. It seemed to us that it would be helpful to present his anthroposophical work to readers—not in the form of some underground publication, but openly and honestly—so that each reader could form an individual opinion based on an unprejudiced reading of what Tomberg himself wrote or said.

Introductory:
The New Michael Community
and its Significance for the Future

*D*EAR FRIENDS:

First, let me say how glad I am to be back in Rotterdam after a year's absence and to see so many familiar faces!

I would like to add that I have just come from the annual Summer School in England where others have been doing work similar to the work we will embark on here. This presents me with the opportunity of forming a personal connection between what was done in Britain and the work and people here. Such connections exist not only when a person relates logically what is done in one place with what is done in another, but also when individuals involved in one place move about and meet those involved in another. The connections then become human, real, and living. In this sense, I would like to try to connect the work just ended a few days ago with the work we are to begin here.

Let me also say that our opening musical presentation was a most wonderful and appropriate prelude to the work we have planned. The themes we have chosen, arising as they do from the inner, spiritual development of humanity, call for an attitude of mind in all respects similar to the attitude inspired by music such as we have just heard.

During this week, it will be important for our souls to regard what is said with a certain openness and inner silence. What is important is not that we take up and immediately grasp and manipulate the content, but rather that we receive it with a certain feeling for its delicate, essential nature.

This evening we shall consider the important theme of Michael and his community. Bluntly, without further ado, we shall put before ourselves the question, Who is Michael in the cosmos? Who is Michael in relation to humanity? In order to answer this question, we must direct our attention first to another spiritual being, the one who in the Bible is addressed by the prophet Ezekiel as the King of Tyre—that is, as the spiritual being whose earthly reflection was the King of Tyre. Ezekiel says to him:

> Thou art an unblemished seal, full of wisdom and fair beyond measure. Thou art in God's Paradise and adorned with all kinds of precious stones, with sardius, topaz, diamond, turquoise, onyx, jasper, sapphire, amethyst, emerald and gold. In the day thou wert created, thy kettle drums and pipes must already have been prepared in thee. Thou art like a cherub that spreads itself out and covers itself; and I have set thee upon the holy mountain of God, so that thou dwellest among the fiery stones. (Ezek. 28; 12-14)

Now, which being is this of whom Ezekiel speaks in such wonderfully beautiful words? Who is this cherub who dwells in God's paradise among fiery stones and has twelve precious stones in his crown? This "cherub"—or cherubim—is the being Lucifer. It is Lucifer who is spoken of here. Indeed, these beautiful, gripping words say that Lucifer was the being who was ordained by God to dwell among the fiery stones. This means that the cosmic role, or station, on the threshold of Paradise—the one taken up by the "cherubim with the fiery sword"—was in fact intended for Lucifer. Lucifer was to have been the Guardian of the Threshold. Lucifer was the being ordained by the All Highest to stand "on the fiery stones" at the "limit of Paradise" and to guard its threshold. But Lucifer committed the wicked deed (Ezek. 28: 16-17) and was expelled from the Holy Mountain of God.

A fundamental spiritual fact, one that we must understand, is connected with the fact of Lucifer's fall: namely, that the Trinity of the Good brings to expression an altogether definite law, the law that the higher principle of the Trinity sacrifices itself to the lower. We see this law expressed, for example, in the Father of the world. For the Father's primal purpose, which underlies the world, is to be replaced upon the throne by his successor, his Son. It is the Father's hope that he will be replaced in his highest dignity by another being. This is what, in the first place, lies at the basis of both the principle of the Good and of any genuine "white" movement on earth. Thus anyone who takes up a definite position on earth wants to be replaced by a successor, an heir. This is the principle of selflessness.

The trinity—or, more correctly stated, the triple *disunity*— of evil presents something quite different. In the case of evil, the successor is the enemy of the predecessor. The being who comes earlier is always threatened with being swallowed up by the one who comes later. Thus Lucifer, who by his fall became a representative of the first principle of evil in the world, hates his karmic successor, Ahriman, because Ahriman strives to swallow him up. In the karmic future, however, Ahriman himself will be swallowed up by his successor, the Asura—the third principle of evil, which has yet to reveal itself.

It is important to be consciously aware that good reveals itself through the fact that the earlier sacrifices itself to the later. The earlier retires, as it were, to grant a place to the later. In the case of evil, the opposite occurs: the being who comes later becomes the devourer of the predecessor.

Now, because Lucifer had to vacate the place in the world allotted to him by the gods, the need arose in the world to protect Lucifer, for a definite period of cosmic time, from being swallowed up by Ahriman. Therefore another being took up the position on the threshold over which Ahriman may not pass. This other being guards the threshold that represents the protective rampart of the spiritual world against Ahriman. Inwardly, this spiritual being has the dignity of a cherubim, because he has assumed the mission actually intended for a "cherub." This being is the archangel Michael. This is the reason Rudolf Steiner began the verse dedicated to Michael with the words:

> Gleaming spirit powers, arisen from sun power,
> spreading your grace upon worlds:
> you are intended by the thinking of the gods
> to form Michael's garment of rays.

What is being referred to here? These lines state that spiritual powers arisen from the sun are meant to form Michael's garment of rays. In other words, Michael is destined for another, higher dignity than the dignity vested in the other angels and time spirits surrounding him. This happened because Michael offered up a sacrifice by putting himself in the empty place, the one vacated by Lucifer.

To understand Michael's position in the cosmos even more concretely, we must direct our attention to another being. She is a being who is quite unknown and is entirely misunderstood in the West, one whose name indeed has barely been preserved. In the Greek-Slavonic East, however, a feeling memory of her still lives and comes to expression in religious art. This is the being who, revealing the unity of the Father, the Son, and the Spirit for human consciousness, makes the Divine Trinity into a *Tri-Unity* for the consciousness of the beings of the world. Therefore she has the following symbol:

If you imagine this being, she will take the form of a circle circumscribed about a triangle. In ancient Israel, Solomon the Wise spoke of her thus: "Wisdom [Sophia] built her house and raised it upon seven pillars" (Prov. 9: 1). Speaking in the voice of Sophia herself, Solomon says:

> The Lord knew me at the beginning of his ways; before he created anything, I was there. I was installed from eternity, from the beginning, before the earth. When the deeps were not yet in existence, I was already born; when the springs were not flowing with water, before the mountains were set upon their foundations, before the hills, I was born. When he had not yet made the earth and what is upon it, nor the mountains on the surface of the earth, when he prepared the heavens, I was there. I was there when he measured the deep, when he fixed the clouds above, when he made firm the springs of the deep, when he set a limit to the sea and the waters so that they should not overstep his command, when he laid the foundation of the earth. (Prov. 8: 22-29)

Sophia preceded all things. She is no mere principle, nor a mere plan for the structure of the world, but rather a true spiritual being who has descended to the hierarchy of the archangels. At present, therefore, Sophia can be regarded as an archangel. An event that may be regarded as a misfortune did, however, occur with respect to the being of Sophia: namely, Lucifer robbed her of a particular capacity. Rudolf Steiner refers to this fact in a verse which begins:

> Isis-Sophia
> Wisdom of God—
> Lucifer hath slain her
> And on the wings of the cosmic forces
> Carried her forth to the widths of space.

It was Sophia's imaginative capacity that was stolen from her. The Sophia being lost her capacity to work into the earth because Lucifer had gained control of the power with which she can unite herself vertically with earthly humanity.

Lucifer appropriated Sophia's imaginative power to himself. This was his "fall"—the crime, the misdeed, of which Ezekiel speaks. Lucifer turned cosmic wisdom into *personal wisdom*; and Sophia's power became *sheer fantasy* for human beings. Fantasy thus became the Luciferic counterfeit of the revelation of Sophia. It became the power of lying. Sophia, for her part, had forfeited the possibility of conveying messages to humankind, of allowing her revelations to flow directly into the being of humanity. She fell silent, waiting for the future moment when she would be able to convey to humankind the gifts with which she is inwardly filled. The image that expresses what makes up the inward being of Sophia, and can be found especially in the East (as well as in the West in a certain form), is that of the *Mater Dolorosa*, the suffering mother. Suffering is the keynote of Sophia's being in the world. She is filled inwardly with unlimited treasures of wisdom, but she is condemned to silence. She would like to bestow her gifts upon all beings, but she is powerless to do so. Thus she gazes upon the generations of men and women on earth, and the suffering that fills her can be compared with the suffering of a mother who is prevented from bestowing gifts upon her children—as she wishes to and otherwise would.

By means of her language of suffering, Sophia is now, in relation to the hierarchies, the *other* Guardian of the Threshold—in the sense that the threshold has two sides. For one can cross over the threshold from two directions: from the spiritual world into the physical, lower world and from the lower world into the upper world. Michael stands at the threshold separating the lower world from the upper. He prevents the powers of the lower world from encroaching into the upper worlds. Sophia is the being who guards the threshold of the spiritual world, preventing unlawful crossing from the spiritual world into the lower world—and thereby ensuring that unlawful revelations from the spiritual world do not occur. While Michael prevents the penetration of the sinful eye of knowledge into the spiritual world, Sophia prevents the unbridled and untimely will-to-revelation of beings of the spiritual world from penetrating into the lower world. How does she do this? How can we come to understand that Sophia withholds revelations from the spiritual world, since it is she who lives in the hope that these revelations will one day be possible?

Insofar as she is the bearer of suffering, who has been robbed of her imaginative power by Lucifer, Sophia is spiritually and morally a warning image for the other beings. She stands there in the spiritual world as the *Mater Dolorosa*, pale and colorless, robbed of her garment of light—a warning to other beings not to fall prey to the temptation that is the essence of the Luciferic. Thus she guards the entities of the spiritual world from Luciferic error, just as Michael protects these beings from intrusion into the spiritual spheres.

We now face the question: How does Michael carry out his mission as Guardian of the Threshold? From a number of Rudolf Steiner's lectures we know that during the course of the year there is a time when Michael's mission comes very much to the fore. This is the period, beginning August 8th and ending in October, when his fight with the dragon takes place. During this period, the festival of Michael is celebrated (29th of September). Rudolf Steiner has shown us, in an imaginative, picture-like way, how this confrontation of Michael with the dragon occurs.

We may now take a step further in deepening our understanding of this imaginative picture, in order to understand Michael's activity from another perspective. What is the significance of the fact that a battle occurs every autumn between Michael and the dragon? This confrontation, which takes place in the region halfway between the earth and the moon, happens in order to frustrate the attempt Ahriman makes every year to gain control of the moon. Ahriman wants to gain the eighth sphere, which is "chained" to the moon, for himself.[1] He would like to obtain a direct connection with this sphere so that it would then be *directly* connected with the interior of the earth. This would mean that the powers of the Virgin who, according to the Christmas Imagination, supports herself upon the moon, would also be dragged into the cycle of earthly events. What Lucifer did in robbing Sophia of her power of *imagination*, Ahriman wishes to carry a stage further, in that he wishes to gain possession of her power of *inspiration*. Every autumn this attempt of Ahriman's is brought to naught by Michael. Every autumn this happens at the "threshold"—for this area between the earth and the moon is the threshold. Over and over again,

---

1. Tomberg considers the eighth sphere in more detail in *Anthroposophical Studies of the Old Testament*, Studies II & IV (Candeur Manuscripts, 1980.)

the "dragon" is hurled back into the "abyss," i.e. into the interior of the earth. Thus Michael fulfills his cosmic mission as Guardian of the Threshold.

Now, as you know from various lectures of Rudolf Steiner, Michael has a *historical* mission. He was the folk spirit of the people of Israel. How are we to understand the fact that this guardian of the threshold could simultaneously be a people's folk spirit? We can understand it by looking at the mission of this people and realizing that they were *themselves* a kind of threshold. The people of Israel, as a community, consisted of "people of the threshold." They bore within themselves the Mystery of Christ and thus they were themselves this threshold. This explains the superhuman severity and strictness with which, in the course of their history, the people of Israel avoided mingling with other cultures. It explains likewise the apparently inhuman, cruel obliteration of the cults of the "high places," and of the "sacrifice of the first born" in fire. This extermination of all foreign spiritual life within Israel was a necessity, for the cults on the "heights" represented a Luciferic trend, and the rite of "Moloch" represented an Ahrimanic trend. The threshold of the Christ Mystery had to be kept guarded. Thus it was indeed guarded, and the guardian was the folk spirit of this "people of the threshold," Michael himself.

During the period between the eighteenth and the beginning of the nineteenth centuries, Michael brought about a mighty and significant spiritual deed in the spiritual history of the world. Rudolf Steiner speaks of this in his lecture cycle, *Karmic Relationships (volume III)*. In these lectures he says that Michael revealed at that time what now, in part, is beginning to shine forth on earth in the form of Anthroposophy. Michael thus performed a mystery act, a cult, before the souls of human beings. What sort of cult was it? What was its content? This cultus was a new creation of the imagination that was stolen from Sophia by Lucifer. Michael recreated it and presented it anew. What Rudolf Steiner meant by "cosmic intelligence administered by Michael" is the fact that Michael was able to make Sophia effective again. What is meant by Michael as "administrator" is that he has again placed in Sophia's service the power through which she can reveal herself. It means that Michael has made it possible once more for revelations to come from the spiritual world through Sophia. That is, he has rebuilt the bridge that reunites Sophia with the earthly world.

The content of Michael's cultus consisted of two aspects. On the one hand, there is everything that can light up as spiritual knowledge through the contemplation of external nature; on the other, there is that which can light up as memory in one's inner life through contemplation of the destinies of individual human beings and humanity. Michael presented the mysteries of nature and the mysteries of humanity's karma in the form of a cosmic cult. To be a "Michaelite" today means to be a person who, through the contemplation of nature, has memories of the cult that one's soul experienced in the time before birth; it also means that, as such a person contemplates the destinies of individuals and of humanity, memories of the cult in which Michael showed the mysteries of human karma are allowed to shine forth. Thus at present a Michaelite is an individual endowed with a special insight into nature and the destiny of humanity. If one sees signs in nature which awaken symbols and images of the cult of Michael in one's soul, then one is contemplating nature in Michael's spirit. And if one observes individuals and their destinies in such a way that deep within one's soul remembrance is awakened of the cult of Michael, of images of the Fall, of the Mystery of Golgotha, of perspectives regarding the future—then one has a Michaelic-solar eye. Such people constitute and represent the Michael Community.

The outward sign of such individuals is that they have a special relationship to thought; indeed, they experience the power of thought, as such, quite differently from other people. They experience thinking in such a way that they do not demand proofs and facts in order to be convinced of the truth of what they have come to know. For they experience thought not as a logical possibility, but rather as *the power of memory of the cult of Michael*. The truth, the feeling for truth, is endowed in such persons with a *magical force*. A person becomes deeply stirred by the power of a thought. One knows that it is the truth, because one's whole soul recalls the might of the cult and therewith the power of truth. It is the power of truth that distinguishes Michaelites from other people. For them, truth is not only something right, but something imbued with magical force.

A special combination of thinking and willing is the distinctive characteristic of the Michaelite. Hence, the second part of the Michael verse runs as follows:

> He, the messenger of Christ,
> Points in you to the holy cosmic will
> That bears the human being.

This cosmic will, which bears and takes hold of human beings, is what streams through Michael's power and presence into human thoughts that are rooted in truth.

The community of Michael must also prove itself in life. It has to show itself to be a special element in life, an element that deserves the same significance in general cultural life as its material counterpart already receives. It must represent a combination of clear thinking and faithfulness to the truth. These must permeate the individual as a will element by the power of inner conviction. Such power of thinking is called "spiritual iron." It is the spiritual archetype of what is found physically on earth as iron. When we encounter individuals who stand up for what they know, for what they have inwardly recognized to be the truth, with an iron firmness, individuals who stand like pillars—giving way neither to right nor left, but who withstand all assaults with dedicated strength of will—then we have experienced a bit of spiritual iron on earth. Every person who stands dedicated to recognized truth is a sword of Michael, and is himself or herself a kind of "guardian of the threshold." Such individuals repel trespassers, just as they draw the honest to the threshold on which they stand. This is the essence of the Michael Community. It must be made up of such individuals.

What sort of future faces this community? The memories awakened in the soul through the cult of Michael become capacities. Given the framework of this talk, it would take us too far to present in detail how these memories become capacities—how they become the new etheric clairvoyance. The new natural clairvoyance will reveal itself among human beings in two ways. Some people will see the spiritual at work in nature, will recognize how the elements are the expression of those spiritual mysteries that have flowed into the earth through the Saturn, Sun, and Moon existences. The mystery of evolution in nature will become ever more apparent to these individuals. In another group, a different capacity will emerge—a karmic seeing, the beholding of the karmic past. They will behold the karma called forth by various deeds. Rudolf Steiner also spoke about this. I should add that the mode of seership of such individuals will consist in their being endowed with a clairvoyance that investigates the karma of humanity. They will remember their own karmic connections, then those of other people, and so on and on.

What tasks will be received by those who belong to these two groups? First, we must indicate what kind of individuals these two groups constitute. Rudolf Steiner speaks of two streams within the Anthroposophical Movement: the "Platonists" and the "Aristotelians." The Platonists are those in whom the new clairvoyance will appear in the form of karmic seership. The Aristotelians will have a clairvoyance with regard to the secrets of nature. The community of Michael will consist on the one hand of people who have developed their consciousness-soul so as to use their clairvoyance to gain knowledge of nature and, on the other hand, of people who will receive the principle of the spirit-self into themselves in order to experience karma.

These two groups must work together, there is no other way for it to be. They will *have to* work together. They will represent the whole, complete circle—the circle of the new, spiritual knighthood—which can bear the name: "Michael-Sophia in nomine Christi." The men and women of Sophia, of revelation, will walk the path together with the men and women of knowledge; the Platonists will stand guard together with the Aristotelians at the threshold of the spiritual world. They will have to guard the secrets of the spiritual world. In this community, guardianship will involve neither keeping silent nor revealing everything. Instead, it will mean that a living rampart, or wall, will be erected—a wall consisting of steadfast human forms who will stand as a vertical connecting link between the spiritual and the physical worlds. On one side they will open the gates to the authorized, and on the other they will close them to the unauthorized. This community of knights—this future community of "knights of the threshold"—will be fully realized in the sixth cultural epoch. It was begun through Rudolf Steiner, through the founding of the Anthroposophical Movement, through the revelation of the mission of Michael, and through the misfortune which we later experienced. We are summoned by the voice of Rudolf Steiner, we are tested by the misfortune now coming to us [1938]. What we must awaken in the depth of our souls is *earnestness* in regard to the spiritual and outer worlds, and *fidelity* to the spirit, each one according to his or her position in life. We can conduct ourselves in every way, in speech and action, according to the demands of everyday life. But let us keep one province free from compromise; let us remain *true to the spirit*, independent of all teachings and teachers, of all organizations in the world. Let us remain faithful to the inner voice of truth and conscience! Then we are in the school that is preparing for the future Michael Community—the community that will bear the motto:

Michael-Sophia in nomine Christi.

Meditation:
Its Being and its Effect

$\mathcal{D}$*EAR FRIENDS:*

We ended our reflections yesterday by speaking of the future of that community of individuals we called the Michael Community. We spoke of this community as consisting of two groups possessing different inner faculties.The difference, we noted, is that those of the one group are more disposed to perceive clairvoyantly the secrets of nature, while the others are more inclined clairvoyantly to investigate the secrets of karma. These two groups are the so-called Platonists and Aristotelians—not in the sense that they represent Platonic or Aristotelian viewpoints, or that they belong in concrete reality to these two cultural streams, but in the sense that those of the one group are more disposed toward the principle of revelation while those of the other are more disposed toward the field of research.

Today we must ask the question, How can the ideal of this community be realized in the world? Here, right at the outset, we must state clearly that although these two groups are inwardly different, the following path of development is equally valid for both. This path is based upon a definite principle—the principle of spiritual exercise or practice. This principle has two fundamental aspects.

The first is the fact that one should not immediately attempt to grasp all life experiences consciously, for in that case one would lose one's natural and unselfconscious openness to life. One must choose a definite time to be completely *conscious*, while continuing to follow the ordinary current of life with natural openness during the rest of the day. The time chosen for spiritual exercise is meditation. Here, for a short period of the day, the intention is to be wholly permeated with one's consciousness, so that nothing arises within oneself that is not determined and created out of that consciousness. The result of these moments of becoming completely conscious is that in the immediate, habitual course of everyday life the wish arises to be just as conscious as one was during the time of meditation. One's body and one's soul become fond of the clarity and brightness experienced during meditation. Not only does the soul begin to yearn ever more for this clarity, but so does the body itself. In this way, presence of mind makes itself increasingly felt in daily life. We could say that one's taste for being conscious, for having oneself in hand, is increased—and this aftereffect then spreads over the whole course of life, so that one becomes calmer, more self-possessed, and more peaceful. The process may be shown with the help of a drawing:

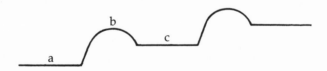

If *(a)* represents the ordinary level of life with which we begin, this is raised by the experience of spiritual exercise *(b)* to a new level *(c)*. And so the process continues, ever further, although the steps may be very small. Thus there exists a connection between the level of consciousness of everyday life and the consciousness achieved during spiritual exercise. The connection consists in the fact that meditation indirectly results in definite powers pouring forth into life, and in the fact that a person learns to appreciate self-control by the exercise of free will. This is one of the principal aspects of spiritual training.

The other aspect lies in the fact that it is not a question of a single great effort, but rather of constant repetition. Rudolf Steiner once coined the formula: "Rhythm replaces strength." This is valid for both physical and spiritual life. At present, the situation is such that slow, gradual efforts can bring a person genuinely forward in such a way that no disorders (*Krankheiten*) will set in, as might well happen when an attempt is made to achieve a great deal in a short time.

These two aspects—the immediate effect on daily life and the rhythmic repetition—are fundamental to spiritual training. Those with artistic or religious feelings, however, might voice certain definite objections to the principle of spiritual exercise itself. The response to the idea of spiritual training by those specially attuned to cultivating insights of an artistic nature, or through religious fervor, may be that spiritual exercise brings something mechanical into life, and that therefore the element of spontaneity and unpredictability in one's inner life can be destroyed. The reply to this objection would be that one's breath is something that always repeats itself rhythmically and that harmonious breathing is the foundation for human health and life. In fact the soul, when it acquires a kind of "breathing" of its own, achieves for the inner life a similarly ordered existence. In truth, therefore, the soul does not become mechanized in spiritual training, but instead grows into an inwardly ordered organism. The chaotic element in the life of the soul may from time to time make flashes of artistic and religious life possible, and yet it is the rhythmical element that makes possible a life of soul in which one is in contact with the spiritual world not just temporarily but *continuously.*

Let us now try to reach a deeper understanding of the nature and essence of meditation. We will first make a picture of the inner state of a person's consciousness in order to understand the changes meditation brings to this condition. I will again make use of a drawing (see Figure 1). If you picture the human inner being as standing before you, then the person's angel will be there above. In principle, anyone can be permeated by his or her angelic being. Anyone can, at present, achieve a relationship with his or her angel. In whatever one can create for the sake of the world that is positive, one may unite with one's angel—to the point of one's very heart—in acts of cognition. On the other hand, a human being's so-called higher I is not completely incarnated. The higher I is something that the angel envelops, just as a mother envelops her child in her womb. When the higher I is born, the angel is freed from human duty and is no longer that person's guardian angel—hovering, guarding, protecting him or her. Instead, the angel becomes a friend—one who walks with the person or even departs, if entrusted with other tasks. The realm of the angel is where the higher I is found—the higher consciousness that exists beyond the threshold of human consciousness.

The brightest point in ordinary consciousness is where we possess initiative in regard to thinking. This is not a dead point, but one that rays out and is in movement. The beams always extend in four directions: upward and downward, right and left. The directions right and left relate to the system of the senses; the directions upward and downward relate to active, independent thinking. The beam pointing downward reaches the sphere of the so-called *subconscious.* This sphere is the element in us that must be influenced by the practice of meditation. The subconscious is not simple; it is complicated, in the sense that present within it are not only very different unconscious instincts, wishes, passions and so forth—but also different beings. It is here, in the so-called subconscious, that one meets the *Luciferic* angel, who, in the fullest meaning of the word, is bound up with the human astral body.

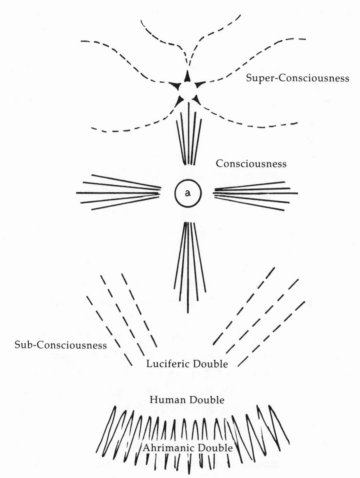

Super-Consciousness

Consciousness

a

Sub-Consciousness

Luciferic Double

Human Double

Ahrimanic Double

FIGURE 1

Fastened to the human astral body, the Luciferic angel's greatest hope is one day to become free of it. This angel is also referred to as an individual's so-called Luciferic double, because it represents a second human astral body bound up with the first. The Luciferic double "fell" at the time of the Fall in the middle of the Lemurian period; since that time this angel has been bound up with the human astral body. Its inner longing is to not exist at all. Instead of being bound up with the human astral body where, in our inner being, it repeatedly causes us to lie, this angel longs to be dissolved into the world's astrality.

Deeper within the human astral body, we encounter the sphere of the purely *human* double—i.e., the purely human subconscious. Deeper still, if we descend as far as the etheric body, we find the sphere of the *Ahrimanic* double. Thus the human subconscious is penetrated with the effect of the activity of the Luciferic angel and its Ahrimanic double: the subconscious is Luciferic and Ahrimanic. Therefore we have a threefoldness: superconsciousness, consciousness, and subconsciousness.

In order to understand the effect of meditation on the whole human being, we must now develop deeper insight into the individual components of the human subconscious. We must understand to a certain extent what the Ahrimanic double is. It is an etheric being who clings to the human etheric body and strives to gain control of the etheric body and the human I. Just as there is an archetype of the human being in the heavens (we find such archetypes in Greek classical art), so also there are caricatures of the human in the subterranean sphere. And just as our angel, standing above us, represents, one could say, our archetype, so it is that the Ahrimanic double, on the other hand, is our *caricature*. This caricature, the Ahrimanic double, is a very intelligent being, one who does not manifest through arousing wild passions, but instead manifests particularly whenever subordination to an aim works strongly in a person. Precisely those individuals, therefore, who are highly respectable (from the external, bourgeois point of view) can be tools of this Ahrimanic double. It is precisely such people who can be subordinated, to a very high degree, to the being of the Ahrimanic double—who thereby takes on the leading role.

If we now ask ourselves what the effect of meditation is, we find it consists in the fact that activity is kindled from this point (see *a* in Figure 1): a person only performs such deeds as are based upon his own free initiative. Other activities in the world are based upon *outward* circumstances. One eats because of hunger, one drinks because of thirst, one works because one must earn money. But nothing in the outward world determines the activity of meditation. It arises from free initiative, from one's full consciousness. What happens, then, when one gives oneself over to meditation? A stream flows upwards to the higher I and to the angel, and a connection arises—consciousness is linked with superconsciousness.

From superconsciousness a stream of light begins to flow downward and it strengthens the downward current that flows into the subconscious. This stream of light that has become highly conscious illumines now the subconscious, purifying it. What does purification of the subconsciousness mean, what does catharsis mean? It means, firstly, that the Luciferic angel is gradually freed by the angel that stands above—that the Luciferic double becomes increasingly freer: it means that the subjective Prometheus bound to our astral body, to the cliffs of our being, is freed of his fetters. This freeing takes place through the growing inner love of truthfulness. When we radiate light into our unconscious with our consciousness, we discover our inner untruthfulness; that is to say, everyone has an inclination towards lying—lying not so much in word, but lying in deed. This inclination toward lying is inwardly destroyed and is replaced by a yearning for truth. This is the loosening of the bonds of the Luciferic angel. The Luciferic angel frees itself from our astral body, becoming a being that can freely move around us, so to speak, in our destiny. Thereby it becomes a servant of the angel.

A second effect of the purification of our subconsciousness through meditation is that the stream penetrates deeper into this human subconscious realm—which is both Luciferic and Ahrimanic. This realm consists, moreover, not only of these influences, but also of our *own* Luciferic and Ahrimanic elements—elements that we ourselves have taken up into our own being. As we progress in our meditations, and the bright stream of spiritual light penetrates increasingly into our consciousness, this element is increasingly expelled from the subconscious.

As this element is expelled from the subconscious, it becomes *conscious*; it becomes, as it were, revealed. Just as a snake discards its skin and the skin lies before it and can be seen by it, so a person sheds the lower I, the astral subconscious, which then becomes a sort of perceptible "double." The more perceptible it is, the better; for one learns in this way to keep it in hand and control it. Thereby one learns, too, to become conscious of the sources from which one's mistakes arise, conscious of how one can commit actions that do not correspond to one's intentions. Indeed, in the case of individuals whose I is weak, this double can become a being who not only accompanies them everywhere, but also acts and speaks with them. A person can utter seven sentences of which one has oneself formed only four, while three derive from the double. In learning to be mindful of this "companion," who would like to slip into every utterance, into every inner judgment, and into the happenings of the outer world, one acquires self-knowledge; one learns to have exact knowledge of one's own being.

Again arising from the purifying effect of meditation, a third aspect—beyond the *redemption* of the Luciferic double and the *exposing* of the human double—is the *driving out* of the Ahrimanic double. This double cannot be transformed within us, but must be driven out, so that the human being loses all connection with it. We must give this double no food—thereby it is forced to retreat before the descending light of meditation, to retreat in the literal sense of the word, as far as our feet. There it clings, as it were, and is dragged in the horizontal dimension through life. Then there comes a moment when it breaks off like a brittle twig, and thereafter the individual is free of the Ahrimanic double. One can feel what has happened in that one's gait becomes lighter: from one day to the next a person's gait is changed. The effect comes from the fact that one is freed from an inner burden that had been bound to one's feet. The falling away of the burden causes the experience of becoming lighter.

Thus, you see, the practice of meditation is not cultivated simply in order to experience the breath of the spirit (*Geisteshauch*) or to acquire any special knowledge. It is cultivated to bring about a profound change in our whole being. The practice of meditation redeems a being in our subconscious, exposes and thereby gives birth to another being for our consciousness, and expels a third being into the world. All this has to happen if a person is to go through the stages of imagination, inspiration, and intuition. Dramatic happenings take place. We must become independent of the Luciferic angel so that we can trust our imagination. We must give birth to a human double so that we can trust our inspirations. And if we remove the Ahrimanic double from our being, then we can experience pure intuition. More will be said about this later. Today our concern is the inner nature of meditation itself.

Until now we have spoken of meditation as spiritual exercise. There is, however, another kind of meditation that must also be repeated rhythmically. This kind of meditation does not have the task of making a connection with the spiritual world, but rather has the task of acquiring knowledge of certain things. There are meditations which are spiritual exercises (*übende Meditationen*), and meditations for acquiring knowledge (*Erkenntnismeditationen*). The latter are undertaken with the purpose of penetrating certain mysteries. This kind of meditation also can be represented diagramatically (Figure 2).

The I poses a question, placing it as high as possible, so that it must rise still higher. In order to raise the question upward, one brings forth from within oneself greater and greater intensity, higher and higher energy: thus the question rises. As it rises, it meets certain beings of the spiritual hierarchies and becomes filled with their inward radiations. Then it returns to the human being where it lights up as knowledge. We have *understood* something.

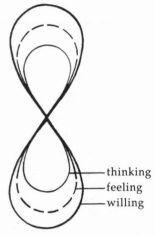

FIGURE 2

One can rest content with this, or one can go further. To go further means that one does not stop at an understanding of the answer to the question, but goes on to experience the full value and content of both question and answer. Then the stream descends into the depths of the subconscious; from there, the feeling and the will of this thought return and may be cognized. Deeper penetration is achieved by posing ever higher questions and receiving ever higher answers. Then the question reaches one's will. The form of this activity is a figure eight, a lemniscate. This process of cognitive meditation is carried out to understand something not only with one's head, but also with one's heart, and finally with one's whole being. For if my whole being has understood something, it means that a definite truth has awakened right into my will.

Thus we can say that, first, the answer penetrates as far as thinking, then as far as feeling, and finally as far as willing (see Figure 2). Meditations that are carried out repeatedly, and are concerned with great cosmic concepts and spiritual mysteries, have as their purpose that an individual, as a total being, be enabled to recognize the total truth of a mystery— not only the rightness of a mystery, but also its life and inner power of truth. Therefore it can be said that a meditation carried out for the sake of knowledge is in accord with the words: "I am the way, the truth, and the life." These words are likewise the stages of meditation—that is to say, a thoroughly Christianized cognition, experienced right into the human blood. All this takes place by means of meditation.

The general effect of meditation consists in the fact that what is spiritual in a human being descends. That is, the superconsciousness—the higher I (see Figure 1)—descends into the human personality, and the angel sends down the helping stream of his illumination in the form of "washing of the feet." Just as Christ bowed down before his disciples and washed their feet, so in every meditation the angel bows down and washes the feet of the meditator. The angel causes the cleansing stream to flow down as far as the individual's feet. This is the image of the Washing of the Feet. For the washing of the feet consists in the fact that the Luciferic angel is redeemed, the human double is exposed, and the Ahrimanic double is driven out. Hence we could say that the spirit thereby bows down, or inclines downward. By means of meditation, the spirit becomes heavier and the soul becomes inwardly radiant. Insofar as the spirit penetrates the soul, the soul learns to "breathe" the spirit. By "breathing in" the spirit, the soul lights up and extends itself; and by "breathing out" the spirit, it ennobles the body. For what is breathed out by the soul enters into the body.

What is striven for, and achieved, by means of meditation is a new relationship between spirit, soul, and body. The spirit approaches the human being, it inclines downward; the soul becomes larger; and the body becomes ensouled. This is the body's inner purification. It becomes pure when everything bound up with its life is permeated by the heart. Nothing in life is ugly if the heart is present. Everything cynical that is said about the life of the body occurs through the fact that those who say such things lack the experience of the soul permeating the body. When the soul permeates the body, the body is raised to the dignity of the soul. Through meditation, a harmony arises between body, soul, and spirit—a harmony that is attained when the spirit inclines downward, the soul expands, and the body is raised to the dignity of soul. What arises before one's inner eye is thus a very familiar symbol, the sign of the Cross. Therefore what is essential in meditation is that one should realize the cross in one's being in a new, *conscious* way. This resulting harmony between body, soul, and spirit is what all human beings in the world, whether they know it or not, call *happiness*. Happiness does not consist in a one's being successful in all one's undertakings, or in one's being surrounded, let us say, by the most beautiful objects. Happiness is a state in which spirit, soul, and body are in inner harmony.

In the whole course of a person's life everything that can be helpful, and that belongs to this inner harmony, is the positive element—the karma conducive to happiness. In the East, in the Orient, people knew the principle of bringing about a balance between spirit, soul, and body. And the superhuman calm, such as radiates from the Buddha in his speeches and in those pictures and images that represent him immersed in perfect peace, is the expression of the actual knowledge of how harmony can be achieved.

But today, now that the Christ impulse has entered into the stream of human evolution, no one can fully experience this peace—this happiness—as long as what is happening among human beings all about one bears within it so much suffering and is the cause of so much suffering. Hence the principle of inner harmony striven for in the epoch *after* Christ is of another kind. It differs from the Oriental ideal. Whereas the Oriental ideal is that the body and the soul should become silent so that only the spirit speaks, for us the ideal is that the soul and the spirit should speak together—in unison—and that the body should yield itself up to this speaking in order that it may be borne out into the world. Soul and spirit speak freely together, and in free will the body follows the current that issues from the spirit.

All three—body, soul, and spirit—become allies and yet work independently, each member according to its own nature. The body is *only* the body, but it loves the soul. The soul is entirely soul and is prompted by no rational motives. At the same time, it is in harmony with the laws of the eternal spirit. Body, soul, and spirit become free—and this freedom leads to an alliance of these three members. When body, soul, and spirit speak and work together, this alliance is expressed. This is the ideal. And meditation is the way that can advance us toward our ideal. Through meditation, higher states of consciousness awaken in us. We will explain later *how* they awaken, and what their characteristics are. At that time we will try to speak of these matters from another point of view.

Indian Yoga in Relation to the Christian-Rosicrucian Path

*D*EAR FRIENDS:

Yesterday we spoke of the essence and effects of meditation. Our approach was that in meditation we see the principle of the washing of the feet at work. We said that by means of meditation the stream directed from above downward brings about the inner cleansing of a human being. The main point that emerged was that the realm of human subconsciousness must be inwardly cleansed through meditation. This purification occurs in definite stages. The first stage is to *liberate* the Luciferic angel, who is bound to the human astral body. The second stage is to *externalize* the human double, whose nature seen from within outward is Luciferic and Ahrimanic—and is thereby gradually to be transformed. We then considered the third stage, the *expulsion* of the Ahrimanic double, who wants to cling to the human etheric body, but—because of the effects of meditative work—finds nothing further to cling to and thereby becomes detached from us. Finally, we tried yesterday to place before us the ideal, the "goal," of meditative work. Here the essential thing is to achieve through this work an equilibrium between spirit, soul, and body in such a way that the spirit inclines downward, the soul is extended, and the body is raised to the dignity of the soul. By this means the three members of the human being, each according to its own nature, begin to speak and work together—so that a kind of alliance comes into being between them, while at the same time each follows its own inner nature. The result is inner harmony, which means true happiness for the human being.

This bringing of the three members of the human being into harmony is exactly what the term *Goetheanism* may be said to designate. When we consider Goethe's significance, it is actually not at all a matter of what he created in the way of a world outlook, nor what he created in the artistic realm, nor the works he achieved in the field of science; instead, what is especially significant about Goethe is that through him a quite definite sort of striving was placed before humankind, a striving which to a certain degree also bore fruit. Goethe exemplified the realization of a relationship between body, soul, and spirit in such a way that each of these three members, out of its own freedom, could create in harmony with the Divine.

Goethe's own words characterize his relationship to the Trinity: "As a man of science, I cannot be any other than a pantheist; as an artist, it is impossible for me to be other than a polytheist; as for being human—that is also taken care of." That is to say, Goethe had no system or dogma before his inner eye. What Goethe had was a threefold inner attitude towards existence. He was *wholly* a scientist and had thus to see in the whole of nature the revelation of the Deity. He was *wholly* an artist and had to recognize the individual qualities of the Divine. And he was *wholly* human—this comes to expression in his novel *Wilhelm Meister*. Although not directly mentioned, the third element in his spiritual makeup was the ideal of Christ.

We can say, then, that in Goethe we are presented not with a teaching about the Trinity, but with a *trinitarian attitude of the soul*. Goethe was threefold in his entire being, and each of these three sides of his being led him to a definite inner comprehension of, and meeting with, the Divine. At the same time one can say that if, on the one hand, Goethe's striving bore fruit in all three of these directions, on the other hand there was also a great deal that was lacking. We cannot speak of Goethe as a *perfect* representative of humanity. And yet we can speak of him as one who clearly, and to a quite high degree, strove toward the ideal of a harmonious human being, and even partially realized that ideal. We have in Goethe, therefore, a striving after a high ideal within a person still burdened with a number of imperfections.

If, however, we turn aside from Goethe and direct our attention to the East, particularly to India, we find human beings who are perfect from the everyday point of view; at least, they are regarded and revered as perfect. At the present moment [1938], Meher Baba lives there. He is called "his divine Majesty" and is much revered. This is because his pupils—and there are a large number of them—are convinced that they have before them a perfect human being. In the East, in India, Meher Baba is regarded as being the epitome of perfection in terms of human development—which is not the case with Goethe, who is much honored, but more honored than understood. Goethe is revered, not because of his perfections, but rather from other points of view, which we will speak of later. For now we will direct our attention to the remarkable fact that there are perfect individuals in India, individuals at least regarded and revered as being perfect. This state of highest perfection, the Mahatma state, which is attained in India by single personalities, is reached by the path of Yoga.

Let us attempt to draw a picture of the essence of Indian Yoga. It is fundamental to Indian Yoga that a force called the "Fire of the Serpent" or the "Fire of Kundalini" slumbers in the human subconscious. This slumbering force is to be awakened. If awakened, it is channelled upward into consciousness and superconsciousness, thereby creating a current that, rising out of the region of the abdomen, ascends as far as the top of the skull, whence it escapes into the outer world. This is a condition of ecstasy in which the soul rises to the greatest heights of the Divine and becomes a Mahatma. The process can be schematically represented (see Figure 3). Imagine the figure of a human being. If the slumbering power of fire (*a*) would be awakened, it would ascend in serpentine movements and then leave the body. It is what the Indians designate as the thousand-petalled lotus flower, the crown center of the head, that is here (*b*) brought into movement, producing a multitude of upward-flowing streams leaving the body. From this the experiences result that belong to Indian occultism.

FIGURE 3

But in fact what really happens later is as follows. The higher the expelled soul life ascends upward, the lower it falls later on—like rain—into the sphere of the Ahrimanic. The physical, natural phenomenon of rain has this process as its spiritual archetype. If an individual ascends, like a cloud, to dwell in the heights, then there occurs after a certain time a fall into the region of Ahriman. Thus Ahriman captures the Luciferic. That is karma. But the impulse lying hidden in this Yoga is not so simple that one can merely say: human beings wish only to be freed from life's vale of tears.

We do wish it, but this is not the essential thing. Let us try to understand what *inner* motives really lie behind the pursuit of Yoga.

When in the life after death one has passed through the cosmic midnight hour, the midpoint in the soul's path after death, then one stands before the possibility of a definite temptation. One says to oneself: "I live in the spiritual; spiritual light surrounds me. It would be possible for me to incorporate into this spiritual light everything that I bear within myself, to unite with it so that everything in me that is imperfect would be transformed into perfection." This is the Luciferic temptation. It means inwardly to break away from, and refuse, the whole further development of *humanity*. In the cycle of lectures Rudolf Steiner gave in Vienna in 1914, *The Inner Being of Man and Life between Death and a New Birth*, you will find a description of these matters. The point is that a temptation can be so great that a human soul cannot withstand it. Such a temptation is therefore concealed by the gods, but nevertheless it is effectively present in the world. The element of temptation here does not consist in one's being offered the possibility of, say, dominion, or of realizing evil intentions, or the temptation of egoism in the worldly sense; no, the possibility offered is that of remaining pure and holy in the spiritual world. But in that case what is imperfect—and yet, as potential perfection, is still present in human nature—will not be developed, even if what is already developed in human nature were to remain forever in the light of purity and holiness. The temptation, then, is to renounce the great ideal of the future. In return, one can attain to a high degree of beauty and light in one's being, insofar as this is now developed.

Thus every human soul stands at one time before the choice of becoming wonderfully holy or else at some time in the future—by working through many, many imperfections—

of attaining a far-off ideal, wherein all undeveloped faculties implanted in human nature by the gods will come to fruition.

Rudolf Steiner speaks of the "temple" of humanity's future as the image of the ideal human being. In the state after death, the soul sees this "temple" and is so inspired by the temple's light that it enthusiastically makes decisions that lead it to return to Earth—in order to attain perfection in a far distant future.

And if a few persons of depth admire Goethe, they do not admire in him the ideal human being, since he is not that at all; rather, they admire the inner power of his striving after the realization of the gods' ideal, his striving towards the temple of which Rudolf Steiner speaks—the ideal of a future humanity whose realization has to occur through the transformation of our many imperfections. On the other hand, in India perfect holiness is admired, and behind this lies a striving that would look upon the present state of humanity as its final state and to renounce all further development of humankind.

Humanity—not human beings as they are, but as they are to become—is the object of the religion of the gods. They have intended a lofty future for humanity. This temple is their great hope, great faith, and great love. The realization of this temple of the ideal human being is the religion of the gods.

Let us now try to understand what kind of temple this is. How can we understand the construction of this temple, which is the archetype of all temples on Earth? In our attempt to understand it, we shall begin from above—that is to say, in trivial language, we shall begin with the roof or dome. The highest idea that human beings at present have is the idea of the Divine Trinity. This has to do not only with the idea of the unity of the three in one, but of three inwardly distinct fundamental feelings. In the case of human beings this can be a matter of three different regions of activity. We should not rest content with having three *concepts* in a unity; rather we ought to be able to bring three sorts of *activity* into relation with the triune divinity in our lives. This is how it is on Earth.

In the future it will one day be different. Indeed, on Jupiter, humanity will have realized the *trinity* as far as the will; that is to say, human beings themselves will be a trinity. Thinking, feeling, and willing will be separate, but shaped into unity by the I. Then, on the future Venus, there will not be a trinity, but rather a *duality*, for the Holy Spirit will be *within* us. We will look only to the Father and the Son. Finally, on Vulcan, we will be at one with the Son. Christ will be in us. We will look up to the Father God only. The future is as follows: if today we have a trinity as our ideal, which to a certain degree will be realized (this is the *Manas consciousness*), then on Venus there will be a duality, and on Vulcan there will be a unity. That is to say, this angle of differentiation, the angle (*a*) (see Figure 4) will disappear; the vault of Heaven will be filled solely with the Father God. This consciousness of standing only before the Father God, who is the highest ideal in the human being, will be the upper element of the human temple of the future.

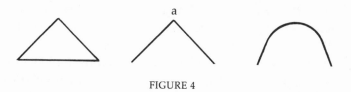

FIGURE 4

Now, the temple roof is supported by seven pillars. These are the paths humanity will have to tread in order to raise itself to this unified consciousness of God. And these paths are in fact nothing other than the stages of the path which Christ Jesus trod on Earth; they are the seven stages of the Passion. In my *Anthroposophical Studies of the New testament*, I tried to depict the seven stages of the Passion as stages of the esoteric Christian spiritual life.

Today, we shall try to consider these stages from the cosmic perspective—for the whole world is the macrocosmic temple which represents the archetype of the microcosmic temple of future humanity. Again and again Rudolf Steiner repeats: "If you would know the world, look at the human being; if you would know the human being, look at the world." As we now have the task of knowing the ideal of the future human being, the microcosmic temple, let us consider the macrocosm and try to understand the temple of the future from this perspective.

The macrocosm, within which we live, began with the old Saturn condition. What, in essence, was this? Its basis was the streaming forth of the will of the Thrones. And this will, which had a sublime origin, streamed downward, forming the lower beings of this world. The beginning of humanity was created. And what was the essential nature of this whole event? It was the same as we spoke of yesterday when we spoke of the washing of the feet as meditation. This streaming forth of the will of the Thrones was the macrocosmic deed of the washing of the feet. Old Saturn is the place of the washing of the feet. This is expressed in the sign for Saturn: ♄. Above we have the cross, which represents self-sacrificial union with the element of passive receptivity, the moon.

If we look next to the old Sun, which followed old Saturn, we find that the Spirits of Wisdom sent forth from themselves the substance of wisdom. This produced the beginning of the life body and of life. What does *wisdom* mean? What does the word really express? We must deepen our understanding of this word. Wisdom, you see, is not a condition of being open to what is *outside* us. Wisdom is the power that streams out from the *interior* of a being in many directions. It is what dwells, actively present, in the interior of the being itself, comprehending its surroundings not in a one-sided way, but *many-sidedly*. If we wish to represent this schematically, we draw a point—for wisdom is contained within the human being. Out of the point, wisdom issues forth in many-sided form. Thus we have the sign of the Sun: $\odot$. This is the expression of wisdom—which is inner and, at the same time, comprises everything. It radiates forth equally in all directions—it is universal. The life force is in fact this striving of the inner being outward toward universality. And the struggle that wisdom, as well as life, must endure in existence consists precisely in the fact that a power must be developed out of wisdom that can put up resistance to one-sidedness, to impact from without, from right and from left. For wisdom is the condition of a being that is capable of relying upon itself, of not needing any point of support, whether from right or from left, of relying upon nothing save its own inner strength of being, and of not being drawn into one-sidedness. This is the power that lives in the principle of wisdom. It was shown in the Gospels in deeply moving portrayal when Christ Jesus was scourged by his fellow human beings. The ability to be centered in oneself—to stand, out of the power of one's own inner being, in spite of all assaults from without—this is the power that is developed through scourging. What constituted the essential heart of the old Sun, what caused the planet to shine forth, was the same power that manifests and endures in the scourging. The planet of the scourging was the old Sun.

And if we now move on to the old Moon, we find the astral element being poured out into existence through the Spirits of Movement. At the same time, this astral element was taken hold of by Lucifer, and a battle then took place in the heavens. *Human karma* began on the Earth, but *cosmic karma* began on the old Moon. We can also put it this way: If the human fall into sin took place on *Earth*, then the cosmic fall into sin took place on the *old Moon*. And as a guardian was placed on Earth to guard the threshold, so also—when the spirits fell—a guardian was placed on the old Moon, one who took karma onto himself. This guardian was the realizer of *spiritual* karma. By remaining true to themselves, spirits received the dignity of the guardian of the divine intentions. The dignity of the guardian is what is expressed by the crown of thorns. The crown of thorns symbolizes a dignity that indeed corresponds to a state of being crowned, but at the same time it wounds the one who is crowned. For the power that the guardian, the representative of karmic necessity, must unfold from within is the power of *inexorableness*. It is the principle of taking a moral stand so that the Truth and the Law will be fulfilled. Pity must be overcome by the being who assumes the guardian's mission. And so the spiritual beings who had to represent the karma of the worlds needed, on the one hand, to look upon the Luciferic being with the greatest pity, and on the other hand they had to repeatedly overcome this pity in order to stand unshakably on the *cosmic threshold*. The power that reveals itself in being crowned with thorns is that of being obliged to judge while experiencing an inward pity that must, however, be constantly controlled and overcome. Thus this crown pricks the wearer himself. And that is what happened in the cosmos during the time of the old Moon. It is the special drama of the old Moon that during this time the crown of thorns came into being in the cosmos.

If we now pass on further to the development of the Earth, we find earthly existence represented by the cross. The carrying of the cross is the fundamental note, the fundamental motif, of earthly existence, and every being connected with the Earth has to experience it in some form or other. During the development of the Earth, humanity must, on the whole, reach the stage of the carrying of the cross; again and again individuals will have to take the cross upon themselves and learn to bear it through the whole cycle, the whole circle, of their experiences. The symbol of the Earth itself expresses this: ♁. The symbol of the circle bearing the cross is the bringing to fulfillment of the carrying of the cross.

During the future Jupiter existence, humanity will have to undergo the experience of the crucifixion. At this stage, humanity will go through those stages of immobility that were originally lived through and suffered by Christ Jesus himself. Human destiny will then essentially consist in the fact that humanity will be bound to the karma of the planet Jupiter and will have to develop a new power out of this middle point, where the lines of the cross intersect each other—a power that will mean the redemption of the Luciferic. And during Jupiter existence the words will cosmically resound that resounded on Golgotha through the good thief. And these words will find the same answer that Christ gave: "Verily I say unto thee, today wilt thou be in Paradise with me." This will happen for Lucifer during Jupiter existence, as humanity itself goes through the crucifixion and loosens the bonds holding Lucifer to the karma of humanity.

And on the future Venus, humanity will have to experience the entombment. This will consist in the fact that the whole of karma, all the realms of nature that are lower than humanity, will be taken up by human beings into themselves, not in the sense of a devouring, but in the sense of a projecting of themselves into an alien (unknown) destiny—in the hope that a cosmic miracle will accompany this sacrifice and that a resurrection of all that is human, which has been laid in the grave, will follow upon this entombment.

This resurrection of all that is human will be experienced by the whole of humankind during the future Vulcan existence. Then humanity will have created and formed the resurrection body which appeared to the Disciples after the death of Christ. This resurrection body will then be the body that human beings will manifest during the seventh stage of planetary evolution.

These seven stages then are the seven pillars of the temple of humanity, the temple of the ideal human being. And to these pillars lead steps that actually represent the states of consciousness in which the seven fundamental tones of existence can be experienced. For existence is a symphony consisting of these seven fundamental, or archetypal, tones. They are the tones of the washing of the feet, the scourging, the crowning with thorns, the carrying of the cross, the crucifixion, the entombment, and the resurrection. These are the pillars upon which divine unity rests and to which four states of consciousness lead—objective consciousness, imagination, inspiration, and intuition. We can experience all seven pillars (the washing of the feet, the scourging, and so forth) in all four realms of these states of consciousness.

Thus we have the picture, which could be diagrammatically represented in this manner (see Figure 5). At the top, we have the human being's spiritual consciousness, which becomes a unity. In the spiritual world we will no longer have *trinity*, but will instead have *unity*. Below this we can imagine seven columns, and these seven columns will rest on four steps leading to the temple. This is the simplest diagram possible, but it represents the fundamental idea of the Temple of the Ideal Human: the ideal state of the human spirit, soul, and body.

This ideal is disregarded by those who follow the impulse that comes to expression in present-day Yoga. For Yoga has the aim of turning all that is not yet perfected in the human being into head—of transfiguring all that is not yet perfected in the same way as the head is transfigured—and then of allowing this head to soar away on angelic wings. One who frees oneself in this way would thus be no representative of

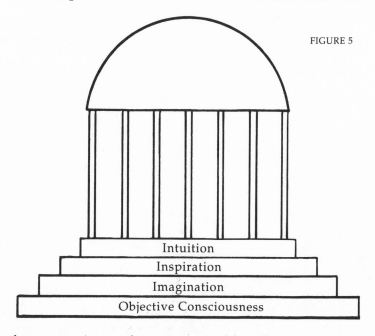

FIGURE 5

Intuition

Inspiration

Imagination

Objective Consciousness

the resurrection: such a person would not have experienced *resurrection*, but rather *deathlessness*. Thus there stand before us two possibilities. One possibility is that of deathlessness and holiness in the present—a holiness that consists in everything undeveloped in a human being becoming head. The other possibility is the ideal of going through the resurrection. It is the ideal of the future, resurrected human being; that is, the ideal image of humanity, of the temple—an ideal that every soul sees after death. Through this vision the soul is fired with enthusiasm to return to Earth to learn the washing of the feet, to experience the power of the scourging, to experience the crowning with thorns; in order, scourged, to carry the cross, to be crucified and entombed and in the end to rise again.

Tomorrow we will speak of the stages of consciousness that are developed on this path.

·

Imagination, Inspiration, Intuition

*D*EAR FRIENDS:

Yesterday evening we considered the difference between two strivings. We considered, on the one hand, that what comes to expression in Indian Yoga tends toward escaping from earthly existence, toward renouncing the gods' aim of realizing the high ideal of humanity. On the other hand, we also spoke of the striving which aspires toward this goal of future humanity—a future ideal which is seen as a reality in the form of a temple by everyone who passes over the threshold into the life between death and a new birth. Then we spoke of the essence of the temple, in that the spiritual striving of human beings in the last epoch of evolution will not be toward the trinity, but toward the unity, the single Godhead. We said that the vault of the temple rests, so to speak, on seven pillars, each of which corresponds to one of the seven stages of the Passion. Cosmic evolution, from this perspective, is made up of the cosmic realizations of the seven stages of the Passion of Christ Jesus. Leading to this are the four steps upon which the temple rests—four steps which represent the four stages of consciousness: objective consciousness, imaginative consciousness, inspired consciousness and intuitive consciousness.

Today we will consider these stages of consciousness in such a way that we will be led to a certain moral deepening. Indeed, it would be meaningless for us to concern ourselves with such matters in a way that does not lead to the intensification of our moral lives.

Let us begin with the first stage of supersensible consciousness, called imagination. This is achieved when one's ordinary consciousness attains a distinctness, a clarity and inner intensity of concentration, to such a degree that *visionary* distinctness is achieved. As everyone knows, you can have a thought which in general you understand and whose significance you appreciate. But you can also have the same thought in such clarity before your mind's eye, its lineaments so distinct, that it becomes visible. The sharpness of the inner focus of attention can be so increased that what takes its course in ordinary feelings and words gains a clarity that leads to an inner beholding of what is contemplated. This is a joyful experience. When one is granted one's first imaginations, one feels oneself strengthened in one's inner being. One feels that the inner illuminating power of one's being has increased, and that as a human being one has thereby become stronger for everything one may encounter in life. One feels awakening in oneself a power that makes possible an all-encompassing perspective of any situation. An inner malleable source of strength has awakened within one, and everything unclear, nebulous, and accidental gives way to make room for what is intentional, strong in character, and clear. This clarification of the inner life leads to imagination. Imagination is not an indefinite living in dreams and fantasies, not a passive taking in of chance images and visions, but rather the clarification of consciousness and the ordering of the life of thought to such a degree that the individual begins to "paint" in spiritual space. This ability to paint in spiritual space is a joyful experience, for one feels one's personality strengthened as a consequence.

With regard to inspiration—or inspired consciousness—the situation is different. It is as follows. Having attained clarity and strength of consciousness, one must extinguish the brilliant, brightly-colored content of consciousness that has been attained. We must renounce the joy of living in the richly filled images that arise before one's inner vision and obliterate the imaginations that have been reached. In their place darkness and emptiness must be created. And in this darkness and emptiness one must immerse oneself with one's entire soul.

The essential characteristic of inspired experience is the condition of inner hollowing-out. The soul feels itself in complete and absolute inner loneliness. One experiences oneself as if forsaken by all human beings and by the gods. The emptiness and absence of everything that could fill the soul grows greater and greater. And although it might seem that one is already quite empty, one experiences nevertheless that one could become still emptier, emptier than one had believed possible. This inner emptying-out is a process of reaching complete inner quiet. The soul becomes so quiet that it hears nothing either out of, or concerning, itself. It reaches the perfect silence of its whole being. And when the soul learns to keep silent in this way, it learns to hear in the spiritual world. Just as when a person speaks, he or she does not hear the other, so if one speaks inwardly (and very often we do speak inwardly), then one does not hear what the world of the soul has to say because one drowns out everything through the noisiness of one's own soul. This experience of emptiness is painful. Every inspiration is preceded by pain, by an enhanced feeling of emptiness—which, however, foreshadows the fullness to come. The emptiness means that the spirit is drawing nearer. One must make room for the spirit in order for it to enter. This making room for the spirit is the emptying of the soul. Full vessels cannot be filled, only empty ones. Therefore, before inspiration, the soul must go through a stage of painful emptiness.

In the experience of intuition, the soul's immersion into the darkness goes even further. It is now no longer just a question of the soul extinguishing outer impressions, remaining in command of itself, and losing all concrete content of consciousness. One must go a stage further. The empty consciousness is also left behind; that is, the soul sinks down into an apparent nothingness, and has the courage to enter, to go further into, this nothingness. A kind of swooning of consciousness occurs at this moment. The soul returns, but returns shone through by memories of this state, transilluminated by new knowledge about the questions that preoccupied it.

The characteristic of intuition is that one is penetrated—shone through—as though by a lightning flash. The characteristic of inspiration is silent listening, the flowing of spiritual insights into the soul. The characteristic of imagination is that one is confronted with vivid, powerful images.

We must admit, however, that such a general characterization does not suffice for a real understanding of this domain. In order to concretely understand imaginative consciousness, we must distinguish three different stages. The first stage is when colors begin to shine forth and forms begin to take shape. These become symbolic. One finds oneself before symbolic images which one can either interpret or not—according to one's abilities. Thus, in the first stage of imaginative consciousness, one stands before the possibility of either answers or riddles.

But more can happen. A person can experience not only images but can be spoken to with complete distinctness and clarity in words, not words such as heard with the physical ear (which would be a pathological phenomenon) but words that are perceived with great clarity in one's soul. Hearing them, one knows that they are not physical words—one knows that they are formed in the sound ether of the world. Words resound within one, and one knows that communications are being offered, not only through images that are either answers or riddles to be interpreted, but in "words" that are spoken to one—words that enrich one's concepts with new concepts. In this way, a person can receive teachings that may contain a whole spiritual course of instruction about specific secrets of the world. This experience is not inspiration, but is rather the second stage of imaginative consciousness. In this second stage, spiritual images become human words. For spiritual images are not only colored, they may also take on a tonal character. Communication in the second stage of imaginative consciousness corresponds to inspiration within imagination.

Further still, it can happen not only that one has symbolic pictures before oneself, not only that one perceives words, but that a being arises before one's inner gaze, a being that is recognizable. One recognizes this being by the gaze that meets one. It is not a question of the form and color in which the being reveals itself. What is important is the content of the gaze. One experiences one's inner eye meeting the gaze of the other being. One senses that one meets this being through the gaze. Through this, the being is recognized. Again, this is not intuition, but rather the third stage of imagination in which, so to speak, the intuitive content of imagination appears.

Thus when we speak of imagination, we must differentiate between three stages. First, there is pure imagination as such. This shows itself in images. Second, there is the language which forms itself inspiringly in words—inspiration within imagination. And third, there is intuition within imagination which occurs when we perceive a being whom we recognize by its gaze.

Much is possible on the path of imagination thus developed. It is possible to have fully conscious communication with beings of the spiritual world, with the dead, and with beings of the spiritual hierarchies. Already at this stage, one is always in a position precisely to distinguish the being whom one meets. If one inwardly experiences a being who has died, then the encounter is always such that the human soul of the person who has died is in a state of continuous movement that must be followed out of inner activity. If one meets a being of the hierarchies, one feels inwardly penetrated as if by an immovable pillar. Through imaginative consciousness, one becomes able to experience facts that one would otherwise never experience—facts of the spiritual world, and facts which the spiritual world can communicate to the physical with regard to events in the physical world, and also facts concerning the Earth's history and concerning humanity itself.

Inspired consciousness is different. It does not involve experiencing new facts, but rather experiencing the *relationships* underlying facts. Nevertheless, as with imagination, we must also distinguish three stages of inspiration.

In the first stage one comes to know secret lines and figures. These are not symbols that have to be interpreted, but rather these are lines and figures in which one learns to recognize the laws of existence. One understands things that are otherwise impossible to understand. That is to say, if one contemplates a spiritual movement from the point of view of inspired consciousness, one finds that the lines lead to the goal toward which the movement is directed. All the facts belonging to the spiritual movement become comprehensible. Such is imagination within inspired consciousness. The forms and lines become figures that have nothing to do with colors and light, but that consist of inner reality and reveal the secret of a definite region of existence. For example, if one contemplates a spiritual hierarchy in this way—if one devotes oneself to a spiritual hierarchy with one's soul, one's inspired faculties—then from within the inmost soul an insight makes itself known in the form of an inner spiritual configuration. One is thus able to recognize what the hierarchy wills in the world, how it sets about realizing this, and what its ideal and goal is. A law is recognized.

The second stage of inspired consciousness is pure inspiration. This shows itself in the fact that one inwardly perceives profoundly unsettling moral tones. We have to imagine the soul looking out into darkness with a definite question in mind. The soul is staggered by what it hears out of this stillness and darkness. That is, out of an emptiness, a darkness, a stillness, the soul learns something that is morally disquieting—something that is not only a fact; but also a moral tone, a resounding word, a communication. This communication, however, does not consist of concepts and facts. Rather it consists of direct communications within the soul. One perceives the word of a being. By means of one's moral faculties, one comes into contact with a higher moral being who can impart understanding for much that is needed in life. One word that a person perceives in this state can result in twenty or thirty lectures needed to express this truth in the language of ordinary thought. Such roughly is the relation of ordinary, everyday, completion-oriented thinking, which acts upon facts, to the inspired experience of the Word, which with one word implants a great truth directly into the soul, a truth which can only be expressed in countless words of ordinary human language. This inner perception of the Word is pure inspiration.

Then comes the third stage of inspired consciousness, intuition within inspiration. Imagine a human being speaking out of himself or herself, either inwardly or outwardly. This person can say what he or she personally thinks, in which case there is no inspiration. On the other hand, a person can try to bring to expression what has been communicated by way of inspiration from the spiritual world, in which case he or she is a mediator. Moreover, it can happen that one brings to expression what one is inwardly perceiving out of the world of spirit as one is perceiving it. This is the condition of co-creation. Here a human being working freely out of himself or herself co-creates the inspiration. This is the experience of inner union. A human and a spiritual being speaking together and at the same time—this is intuition within inspiration. In intuition within inspiration one meets a being with whom one actively works together, and by whom one is inspired in one's will because of this being's immediate influence in one's heart.

Moving up to the third level of supersensible consciousness—to intuition—we must again distinguish three stages. When one's soul returns out of the darkness, the memory of that experience emerges through lightning flashes of warmth and cold. The inner warmth and inner cold tell one of the reality in which one was submerged. What these tell is not unclear—it is the physical experience of warmth that is not clear. Indeed, the experience of inner warmth and cold can be brought to such a distinctness that one experiences a lightning flash of warmth as the immediate recognition of a being in its essential nature. Thus we can speak here of the imaginative stage within intuition. That is, at this stage of intuitive consciousness, imagination makes itself known through warmth and cold.

The next, inspired stage of intuitive consciousness is the experience whereby a person is inspired no longer through warmth and cold, but through lightning flashes of deeds. Here, we can say, the human being experiences deeds as such—the spiritual deeds of spiritual beings.

The third stage, pure intuition, is that of becoming conscious of the fact of one being living into another. For example, the angel can be within the human I, or one human being lives with his or her essential being within the essential being of another. These inwardly become one and live within one another—so that not only do communications pass from one to the other—not only are deeds carried out—but one being is truly within another as a unity. We can understand this if we consider that human relationships can also undergo a change that corresponds to this stage. In objective consciousness, a person is only a fact. If, however, one becomes interested in this person as a soul, then his or her outward manifestations become an expression of the imaginative stage which reveals the psyche. But if one speaks with another in confidence so that this other imparts something of him- or herself, then the relationship is a moral one and corresponds to the inspired stage. Finally, if one experiences friendship, then a deep inward connection, corresponding to the intuitive stage, is experienced.

What I have given here merely as an example can reach stages in the region of the occult that go far beyond what one can experience in ordinary life. In the world of the spirit, friendship can mean something that amounts to a completely different life. An intuitive bond or connection can occur. That is, another soul can walk in a human being on the Earth.

These faculties of imagination, inspiration, and intuition are attainable not merely so that a person may commune with the spiritual world, but also so that things of value may flow into human life through this communion. Indeed, the results of reading the Akashic Chronicle belong to those things that are valuable for human life on Earth. For the Akashic Chronicle is the memory of the world. Just as human beings have memories, so also does the world have a memory. With the help of imagination, inspiration, and intuition, a person can draw upon the memory of the world. The Akashic Chronicle can be seen, heard, and touched. To decipher it requires the faculty of intuition developed to its highest stage. This stage is generally attained only by the highest initiates of humanity. Such initiates can not only read, but also decipher. To decipher is something quite advanced—far more advanced than one could imagine at first acquaintance with this problem. For this deciphering, a faculty must be developed by which one is able not only to unite oneself with the Akashic Chronicle, but also—having returned from one's sojourn there—one must use this faculty to reconstruct in one's normal consciousness all that one has deciphered. This is an enormous achievement.

More often, however, it can happen that a person (through imagination, inspiration, and intuition) experiences the Akashic Chronicle and its parts by being told of its contents by those who can decipher it—beings of the hierarchies or those who have died. Such is the case far more often than is realized—for example, in the case of different discoveries in history, when individuals near the threshold, so to speak, of their consciousness, have experiences. In this way people have made scientific discoveries because parts of the Akashic Chronicle have been brought to them through imagination, inspiration, and intuition. The fact that human beings understand these parts, the fact that the work of deciphering is done for them—all this is of great importance for human knowledge and requirements.

What is of the utmost importance—and concerns and affects all humanity—is a quite specific field of experience, one that can approach human beings through the path of imagination, inspiration and intuition. This field of experience is a very special portion of the Akashic Chronicle. It is not the part that can be found above in the world of Devachan, but rather that which is inscribed in the etheric aura of the Earth itself. This remarkable part of the Akashic Chronicle—which is near to the physical world and may be experienced by us if we devote ourselves to the content and problems connected with it—is present on Earth in the etheric realm. This portion of the Chronicle concerns all humanity. It is the most important truth that human beings can experience and that every human being must experience.

You see, dear friends, when one dies, one has before one a tableau of one's past life. This reveals to one the picture of one's whole life. At the same time, however, this tableau also conceals the sphere of the subterranean, of evil. Thus we are protected from the terrible sight of the subterranean sphere. For everyone in the hour of death stands at the abyss of the Ahrimanic, and the sight of this abyss is hidden by the sight of the tableau which those who have died have before them.

Now, it so happened that once in the history of the world, 1900 years ago, a being died differently from the way in which all human beings have died and still die today. Christ Jesus renounced the contemplation of his tableau and descended consciously into the darkness of the subterranean realm. That was his descent into Hell. He gave his life tableau over to humankind. When, after death, a human being looks upon the tableau of his life, he or she experiences joy in it. Then the angeloi, archangeloi and archai receive it. Christ Jesus renounced his tableau and gave it, not to the angels, but to humanity: at first to the disciples, the sages, and the initiates, but then and essentially to the whole of humanity. This tableau of the life of Christ Jesus is inscribed in the etheric aura of the Earth. It is the "Fifth Gospel," of which parts were communicated by Rudolf Steiner in lectures. For this reason the written Gospels may be lost, but access to the Gospel is always assured to humanity, for the indestructible Gospel is there! Through their own contemplation, human beings will, themselves, be in a position to live through and experience everything that belonged to the Life and Passion of Christ Jesus. And that is the most important task for which imagination, inspiration, and intuition are necessary.

This "Fifth Gospel" contains the entire mystery of the Cosmic Word in images, inspired words, and intuitive possibilities. What the writer of St. John's Gospel said, "The Word became flesh," is a reality. The Cosmic Word, the fundamental mystery of the world, reveals itself in the course of the life of Christ Jesus. We can become initiated into all the mysteries if we experience the life tableau of Christ Jesus. We can experience there, among other things, two definite mysteries— the mysteries of the two guardians of the threshold, the lesser and the greater—in the form of the Temptation in the Wilderness and the Agony in the Garden of Gethsemane.

Tomorrow we shall speak about these things. We shall speak of the mystery of the Temptation and of the mystery of the Agony in the Garden, and how they are connected with the two guardians of the threshold.

The Two Guardians
of the Threshold

$\mathcal{D}$*EAR FRIENDS:*

Yesterday, we took as our topic the stages of consciousness called imagination, inspiration, and intuition. Our considerations culminated with our asking what is of primary significance with regard to this series of higher stages of consciousness. We found our answer in the fact that the tableau of the course of Christ Jesus' life is inscribed in the Earth's etheric aura. For Christ Jesus' life tableau has not been given over to the spiritual hierarchies, has not been transferred to the spiritual worlds, but has remained here in the closest vicinity. Moreover, this tableau contains the collective wisdom of this world in condensed form. For if the Cosmic Word became flesh, then the life of this Cosmic Word become flesh was a revelation of its inner mystery. We spoke yesterday about the fact that two scenes of this tableau are of quite special importance: the scenes of the temptations in the wilderness and the night in Gethsemane. Let us then begin today by attempting to understand the scene of the temptation in the wilderness from a new point of view.

If we consider modern intellectual life, we can see it as a working together of the three currents of science, art, and religion.

Looking first at contemporary religious life from a moral-spiritual point of view, we can see that it is not as pure as it ought to be. It has departed considerably from Christ Jesus' formula for the religious life, "My kingdom is not of this world." Indeed, in religious life today, the "kingdom of *this* world" is so strongly emphasized, that we can justifiably say that religion has succumbed to the temptation of reckoning with the Prince of this world. This corresponds to the first temptation in the wilderness. For, as you will remember, the first temptation was as follows: the world and its glories were shown to Christ Jesus and were promised to him, if only he would recognize the central figure of the world as such—that is, if only he would remain faithful to a center, a point, in the glory of *this* world. And we can say that the temptation to organize the world with the help of a power principle and take possession of it with the help of a central-ized power organization definitely plays a role in history, a role that has led not only to catastrophes of the soul and the spirit, but to bloody wars. If, for example, we consider the history of Rome, then we must admit that in the religious domain Rome wished to be the center that would rule over "the world and its glories." Thus we can say that Roman Christianity (and Roman Christianity is only representative, the other forms of Christianity simply follow in its footsteps) strove to bring the world and its glories under its dominion.

Considering next the cultural stream of contemporary art, we find something in the whole life of art that often leaves a spiritually striving individual unsatisfied. Namely, we find that artistic creation is increasingly becoming a situation whereby the artist creates out of the deep, dark underworld of his or her *subconscious*. The artist leaps from the "pinnacle of the temple" of clear consciousness into the sphere of impulses, instincts—whence something is supposed to arise that is to be regarded as angelic revelation. We can say, then, that contemporary artistic life expresses to a very high degree the succumbing to the second temptation in the wilderness—the temptation to throw oneself down from the pinnacle of the temple to "test" whether God will send his angels to rescue us.

If we now direct our attention to the life of science, we come to an attempt made on a grandiose scale "to turn stones into bread"—which is the third temptation. After all, modern science is based upon the conception that the dead mineral world can be the foundation of everything, and that everything living is only a consequence of movement in this mechanical, dead world. That is to say, all bread arises out of stone.

Thus the content of the three temptations in the wilderness can be found not only in the Gospels but also, if we consider it in an unbiased manner, in the whole of our cultural life.

Three temptations, therefore, live in the history of the world. There is no need to go out into a wilderness; the "wilderness" of our culture suffices for the experience of these temptations. For example, if there is a strong inclination among a people to acknowledge in a single personality the realization of the highest power principle, to see the blood as the expression of the highest revelation of human and divine wisdom, to consider the soil as decisive for determining human destiny—then in this striving for the absolute leadership of one, for revelation through the blood, and for the destiny-determining content of the soil, we have all three temptations *simultaneously.* For to look downward upon the soil as the primary and determining element instead of looking upward to heaven is to transpose the human gaze in the direction implied in the turning of stones into bread. The stones lie below; bread grows from the power of heaven. If one concedes primacy to the soil, then one has agreed that stones should be turned into bread. And if one sees in the blood what should guide human beings, if one seeks one's inspirations there, then one declares oneself inwardly in agreement with the second temptation—namely, the temptation to dive down from the "pinnacle," the highest point of consciousness, into the murky sphere of the blood. And if one is inclined to recognize the highest principle of power in a single personality, then this inclination is the expression of inward assent to the proposition that was put to Christ Jesus by a particular being—to give him all power and glory if he would kneel down and worship this one being.

Thus the present stands under the sign of the three temptations. Indeed, one can best understand the present [1938] by considering it from this perspective. Morally this is the most practical, and at the same time the deepest, way of understanding the world today.

These three tendencies to assent inwardly to the three temptations in the wilderness live in human nature as a whole. And what we call world history is essentially nothing other than the continual karmic confrontation of humanity with the first, the second, the third, or all three temptations. Thus there were periods during which it was a matter of the first temptation; others in which it was a matter of the second; still others in which one had to deal with both temptations; and critical times in which all three temptations appeared simultaneously. We live in an era in which all three temptations appear at once.

As anthroposophists, we can understand why this is so. Because we live in the time in which the return of Christ is to take place, it is, as it were, natural that hindrances in the form of the three temptations should also draw near—not to Christ Jesus, but to humankind. Human nature is permeated by the forces of these three temptations and human karma is the confrontation with them.

For example, when Goethe in *Faust* presents Mephistopheles as a "mixed" character, with both Luciferic and Ahrimanic elements appearing simultaneously in his make-up, this is because it was Goethe's karma to have to deal with the second temptation—that is, with the simultaneous appearance of Lucifer and Ahriman. In other words, it was specifically from the point of view of the second temptation that Goethe created the character of Mephistopheles as the one who brings up the temptation to plunge from the "pinnacle" into the abyss of the unconscious.

In the light of the temptations, then, we can understand not only the most essential trial of Goethe's life, but also the essential trials of other personalities, whether great or unnoticed—for everyone must face and deal with the three temptations. However, if one approaches the spiritual world across the "threshold" that is guarded by the "Guardian," then one has the task of recognizing the forces of the three temptations in one's own being and of ridding oneself of them. This means leaving them on *this* side of the threshold while one's consciousness is still on the *other* side. For this, one must become free of the body in one's thinking (thinking must become "body-free"); feeling must become free of the influence of chance; and willing must be cleansed of the lust for power.

If, for example, one were to carry lusting after power across the threshold and into the spiritual world, one could thereby bring about tremendously destructive effects. For the will is strengthened to such a degree in the spiritual world, that it manifests in ways of which a person in the state of consciousness on this side of the threshold has no inkling. Therefore the Guardian of the Threshold stands on the threshold and shows us our double. That is, the Guardian shows us our subconscious, *reveals* it to us so that we have before us an unerring and true picture of the extent and inner constitution of all the powers that we carry within us—powers that entangle us in the three temptations of existence. If we are brave enough to withstand this sight without despairing over our own nature, without losing all courage so that we become, as it were, living ashes—if we have the courage to endure this truth—then we can cross over the threshold. Transformations then occur within our thinking, feeling and willing.

Indeed, one's thinking becomes something quite different from what it was before. Until then, if we reflected upon something in order to draw logical conclusions, our thinking flowed onward from one thought to the next. Now it becomes transformed into a stream directed upward. A thought becomes a question that ascends to the hierarchies. Through our being we experience meetings with the hierarchies and with persons who have died—then we return with the answer and recall it upon awakening in ordinary consciousness. Thought becomes an answer. The power of thinking becomes the power of vertical memory.

Feeling, for its part, is transformed. It becomes no longer the expression of what one feels with regard to *oneself*. Instead, it becomes an ever-widening circle that takes up not only what one has in one's soul as impressions and sensations from *without*, but also what lives as missions and tasks within other beings. Rudolf Steiner, for example, stood in such a relationship to the dying, mentally ill Friedrich Nietzsche. In *The Course of My Life*, Steiner recounts that Nietzsche's "boundless soul" hovered over his head and that as a result of this impression he [Steiner] took the task of Nietzsche's soul into himself and carried it further. In this way, Steiner took into himself not only the missions of both Goethe and Nietzsche but also what was unfulfilled in Schroer's task. I believe I can say with certainty, moreover, that what Rudolf Steiner took on in the interests of other souls was not limited to these individuals. This is precisely the capacity into which feeling can be transformed—the ability to take up into the circle of one's soul the destinies of other beings and other people.

Now, what happens to the will in one who has passed the threshold is that it raises itself up and becomes a flowing stream in the spiritual world. This process of the will rising up and becoming a stream in the spiritual world, is like the movement of forming a *T*. From the inner, moral point of view, this means that the will surrenders to a stream of time and becomes one with what flows into the future. When this occurs, one experiences oneself in one's will as being engaged, included, in the great task of the spiritual world. The will then is a bridge leading from what was previously willed to what will be willed in the future. For this reason, among all "white" occultists it is a law that no one may come forward in his or her own name, but that one always makes smooth the path for another who is to follow.

In white occultism, a human being and his or her mission are never ends in themselves. One has always to be aware that one is a bridge linking previous strivings with those of the future. Such changes in a person's soul forces signify the passing of the threshold. The power to withstand the first temptation in the wilderness is, in fact, the spiritual faculty that we have been trying to understand here. This power is expressed in the washing of the feet, for the inner strength that reveals itself through the scene of the washing of the feet is precisely what overcomes the lust for power.

The inner strength that allows us to resist the second temptation—the temptation to plunge into the subconscious and to entrust oneself to it—is the power expressed in the scourging. For human consciousness is made up of the effects of Lucifer and Ahriman, both of whom assail us. In the midst of this assault, however, we must create a stream of pure spirituality and stand poised, giving way neither to left nor to right. Such standing firm is faithfulness to consciousness. A firm stance in consciousness is the power that is tested through the scourging. One may be drawn to the left and to the right by the Luciferic and Ahrimanic powers, but if one does not give way, then blows lose their effect. Such is the case both in the inner life of meditation and in outer life, if one is at this stage of development in the unfolding of one's destiny.

The power to resist the third temptation is expressed by the image of the crowning with thorns. To understand this, we must consider that the crowning with thorns means that a person has received a certain dignity (*Würde*)—a dignity received from the Guardian of the Threshold. One who has experienced the meeting with the Guardian of the Threshold becomes to a certain degree entrusted with the Guardian's mission. This mission means standing fast—not giving way a single step either forward or backward. It means standing firm, facing a world that looks upon this guardian dignity as something laughable and unworthy. *Fear* and *shame*, which live in the human subconscious, are covered up in the presence of one who stands thus. Indeed, fear and shame wish to remain hidden. Hiding behind an acuteness of perception approaching clairvoyance, they perceive the *imperfections* of one's personality and the *contradictions* of one's statements— in order to have the right to say inwardly: the truth you stand for is presented unworthily and is therefore an *unworthy* truth. To have to stand thus before shameless eyes that undress one, before ears that almost clairaudiently listen for the negative, is to stand in the position of one crowned with thorns. It is to be invested with a dignity that of itself is wounding, stinging.

To endure the crown of thorns one must have the strength to overcome not only pity for oneself—for one must be firm with oneself—but also pity for one's fellow beings whom, out of compassion, one would like to spare from the uncovering of the truth that arouses shame and fear.

To expose illusions for what they are is very difficult, because it inflicts wounds. People love illusions and wish to have them because they are consoling and they grant the possibility of being at peace with oneself. A measure of severity is indeed necessary to present truths to the world. And this is something that one *must* summon up if one wishes to represent the truth. This severity is precisely the element that manifests the strength needed to overcome the temptation "to turn stones into bread." For the temptation to turn stones into bread does not arise out of lust for power, or the wish to plunge into the unconscious; instead, it appeals to human compassion. Dostoyevsky understood this well in *The Brothers Karamazov* when he showed how the Tempter tempts Christ by saying, "Human beings are hungry. They need bread. You could satisfy them. Then they would no longer need to work and therefore would be appeased." But Christ Jesus rejects this proposal in order that humanity should have to work further by the sweat of its brow and be exposed to need and work. Yet behind this severity stands genuine love, which for the sake of truth must often overcome pity. The strength to overcome pity, when truth requires it, is the power that withstands the third temptation in the wilderness. When one becomes a guardian of the truth that is behind the threshold, one also becomes thereby one's brother's keeper. One acquires an inner attitude toward others that stands in contrast to the words accompanying the first murder, the fratricide of Abel by Cain—for Cain did not wish to be "his brother's keeper."

The path to initiation depends upon a person making the commitment to become "my brother's keeper." Thus when one has become the guardian of the spiritual—of the truth— the next step is to become the guardian of one's fellows, the keeper of one's brothers and sisters. This means carrying the cross. Then one not only carries the burden of one's own destiny, but one also carries the burden of other people's destiny. To carry the cross is to resolve to be one's "brother's keeper."

Proceeding further, we come to a stage of the inner path in which the scene of Gethsemane arises before our consciousness. What is it that is actually so deeply moving in this scene? It is the loneliness of a figure in the garden between the silent, dark heavens and the sleeping men nearby. The loneliness is the essence of the picture.

In order to understand this image, consider the following. When we advance on the path of spiritual discipleship, we ourselves notice very little of this advance. Other people and higher beings notice it, but not we ourselves. We may be well aware of our mistakes and weaknesses, but it is not possible for us to know what we attain in the positive sense. Even the gods had to withdraw from their task and rest on the seventh day so that they could know that the world they had created was good. All the more so are human beings unable to say whether there is progress in their inner spiritual development. There is a sign, however, that does indicate this. It is the fact that one becomes inwardly ever more isolated. At first, one has many companions of the same disposition, awake to the same questions and concerns. Then one discovers with dismay that the circle of people interested in these questions becomes ever narrower. Finally, one finds that there are only two or three others who are still awake in this domain—the others are asleep. At some point a person makes this discovery. Then there comes a moment at which one finds oneself *alone* between sleeping humanity and the dark, silent heavens. During the hour of the greatest decisions, heaven is *silent*—that is a law. The spiritual beings do not want to impel a human being to any decision. As

human beings, we must decide for ourselves, out of our freedom, everything that determines our destiny, our path. And
one can say that this situation—which was experienced to a
tremendous degree by Christ Jesus—must be suffered
through in some form or other by everyone on the path of
spiritual discipleship.

This Gethsemane situation is the step that leads to the crucifixion. The crucifixion is not the experience of being *spread
out*, but is rather the experience of being *nailed down*. It is preceded by the trial, the ordeal, that is expressed in the scene of
Gethsemane, because from one's inner crucifixion—and this
is the intuition—one must pass through the sphere of Ahriman and recognize the rigidifying powers of the world. One
has to penetrate through the powers of sleep, through that
which makes people dull and unaware with regard to everything that should be of concern to them spiritually.

The image of humanity in a state of rigid sleep with
regard to higher questions is a situation that one has to experience. But one must also experience these powers *in oneself*,
as *fear*. Sleep and fear are the expressions of the power of
Ahriman in the world. Through them a person recognizes
Ahriman, not only as Ahriman comes to expression in the
course of events, but also in his gaze.

On the Cathedral of Notre Dame in Paris there is a statue
called "Le Diable Penseur" (the contemplating Devil, the
Devil lost in thought), which portrays a figure looking far, far
into the distance. And what is expressed in this figure? What
is it that appears? Hate, or passion, or fear? No! Out of this
figure there emerges into view an expression of endless,
unfathomable, cosmic boredom—and this is actually the
secret of Ahriman. Ahriman knows what is to become of
everything, including himself. He knows that his downfall
has been decided upon, and that he must nevertheless continue to work as he has worked. Ahriman sits where he sits

and everything is known to him. The numbness that exudes from him in the world is inwardly the power of endless weariness, endless boredom. This power evokes fear in us, but is not fear itself.

If we encounter and experience the rigidifying, benumbing power of the world and yet resolve to stand firm, confronting Ahriman in a manner as immovable as he is—though not out of weariness and boredom, but rather out of faithfulness and love towards the Earth and humankind: this is crucifixion.

The resolve to face Ahriman with the same outer rigidity as he has, while inwardly being steadfast in loyalty to the spirit, is the other sign that can be placed over against the motionless stone *Diable Penseur*. The power of rigidity is confronted by steadfast loyalty to the love principle of the world. Resolving to take this attitude, one encounters the "great guardian of the threshold." This is the Guardian who was first crucified cosmically—Plato already knew of this when he spoke about the "world cross"—and was later crucified in the flesh. This is the one whom we meet as the great Guardian of the Threshold of the temple of humanity.

The first guardian is the guardian of the mysteries of the spiritual world, of the hierarchies; the second guardian is the guardian of the entrance into the temple of humanity, the one of whom we spoke a short while ago. He is the guardian of the ideal of the humanity of the future—not in the sense that knowledge of this ideal is guarded—but in the sense that its *realization* is guarded.

In the meeting with the first guardian, it is a question of knowledge of the truth. In the meeting with the second guardian, what matters is the realization of the ideal of humanity. In this case it is a question not of knowledge, but of deeds, action. And when one has met the great Guardian of the Threshold, then in a certain sense one becomes oneself a representative of the Christ impulse in the world. Becoming such a representative means standing in inner steadfastness, as though nailed to a post, and at the same time it means enabling the call of conscience to resound through the world—awakening it.

Tomorrow we will speak again, from another point of view, about the path that leads to these events and experiences, and I hope that facts of a more concrete and specific nature will thereby come to light.

The Occult Trials

*D*EAR FRIENDS:

Yesterday evening we considered the stages of the Christian-Rosicrucian path of initiation. We spoke particularly of the two fundamental experiences on this path—the meetings with the two guardians of the threshold. The important thing here was to depict the inner drama, as it were, of the path.

Today, I want to begin by giving the practical foundation to yesterday's discussion. This I will do with the help of Rudolf Steiner's book, *Knowledge of Higher Worlds. How is it achieved?* I am sure you all know about the so-called "six exercises," which pertain to the fundamental, indispensable tasks that a student on the spiritual path of inner development must undertake. They are discussed in both *Knowledge of Higher Worlds* and *Occult Science—An Outline*, and they belong among the most basic of meditative tasks.

The first exercise is the control of thoughts. Here a person must develop the utmost strength of thinking in connection with an object that is uninteresting. This involves building up all the thoughts connected with this indifferent object—without the object in question itself summoning forth this power. Practicing this leads to the development of a "muscular strength" of thinking. This strength, this power, manifests itself in that gradually one not only feels one has one's thoughts under control—so that one can place and order them at will—but one also feels a courage-like inner power streaming into oneself. A kind of courage for cognition is born.

The second exercise is the so-called control of actions. In this case it is a matter of carrying out, at specific times firmly set by oneself, actions that are absolutely unnecessary and that are performed only for the reason that one is thereby carrying through one's own resolve. Like the first exercise, this exercise also has a quite specific consequence. One acquires the feeling of having oneself in hand, of being able to order one's thoughts at will despite every hindrance and temptation to arrange them differently. A power of self-control thereby streams into the human organization.

The third of these six basic exercises is the control of feelings. This consists in learning to govern one's feelings in such a way that one is not unduly influenced by either joy or sorrow. One experiences joy and sorrow, but at the same time one finds the strength to face these feelings, to look at them without being drowned in them. Here the power of self-control is extended to the feelings.

The fourth exercise is that of positivity, of developing in oneself the ability to perceive the positive element in all things. It is a matter of finding—by means of quite definite efforts—something positive, good, or beautiful in things toward which one has a negative orientation.

The fifth exercise concerns openness, or trust. One practices looking at and listening to all things and events with complete inner silence, extinguishing all of one's previous experience.

The sixth exercise is that of balance, or inner equanimity. It requires being able to carry out, simultaneously, all the above five exercises in their sequence. Thus it is a matter of mastering the "keyboard" of all five exercises and uniting them in a sixth. This brings about the balance in question.

Such are the six exercises. We can ask ourselves why these six exercises are fundamental and why they concern—and are indispensable to—beginners as well as advanced pupils. In order to answer this question, we will now consider the path a pupil must follow, above all from the point of view not of the *stages* of the path, but rather of the *trials* one meets on it.

If one has been inwardly active at the stage of preparation and purification for a sufficient length of time, sooner or later there approaches the trial of the encountering the "Guardian of the Threshold," which is also called the *trial by fire.* Consisting of shame, this fire is an inward expression of the awakening conscience. A person on the path must go through this fire. It is a matter of recognizing one's own lower nature standing before oneself in undisguised form. This is the "double" that one has generated and expelled. To look in this way upon one's own human double, undisguised, is a trial of courage. To pass through it, one must find the strength not to despair over oneself. One must find the courage not to despair over one's karma. Inwardly one must find the courage to say to oneself: "You are this. This is how you are! Nevertheless, you will always strive to do all that you can to purify your lower nature, to transform it into good. Should it require thousands of years, you will do it—and be certain that you will be able to achieve it." The task is immense. One can shrink back at the enormity of it. It may seem impossible that one could ever accomplish this task with human powers. Nevertheless, one must say to oneself, "I will do it, and I want to do it. I will bring it to completion."

Such strength does not arise from the view of what has stood there, confronting oneself. This strength can only be drawn from the power of the human I itself. No inspiration can be of help, nor can one derive help from thoughts and memories. One must find one's own power of courage. This power has nothing to do with wishes and feelings, but is based solely upon the strength of one's I. The I is strong because it *is*. No help is to be counted upon. The I must prove itself to be courageous. And this trial by fire is actually the *test of courage*. In the process, one does not merely go through a trial; one also goes through an experience—the experience of the birth of a high degree of courage, a courage of which one previously did not know. This courage is the power that gives rise to imagination. It is needed in order to "paint in spiritual space." That is the reason one must develop courage for imaginative consciousness. The content of the trial—facing one's own inner nature—makes it possible to distinguish imagination from illusion. One is then aware of the sources of illusions, and can exclude them.

Having passed the test of courage, the soul then enters into a state of no longer having firm ground upon which to stand. The situation is such that the human soul is surrounded by endless possibilities of movement—in all directions, simultaneously. Immersed in the realms of a myriad influences and evocations directed toward it, the soul can surrender itself, engage itself with a thousand things. A power must therefore be created that keeps the soul steadfast and gives it a sense of direction. The soul must develop out of itself the ability to renounce the abundance of spiritual influences. It must become able to restrict itself to one option among this abundance of possibilities. This is at once the trial of self-control and the experience of it. And self-control is necessary for inspirational knowledge. For inspirational knowledge is based upon one's increasing capacity to bring oneself to a state of quiet—to exercise control over oneself to the extent that one has oneself in hand, completely still and silent.

If one goes through this trial by water—if one develops self-control—then one's soul enters into a region of destiny where one not only has no ground beneath one's feet and must find one's own direction by a kind of "swimming"; the soul also enters here a space devoid of air. One enters into an utter loneliness and wilderness of soul life. The impulses of thinking, feeling, and willing cease. One's soul is like a sailing ship standing with sagging sails in windless weather. It enters into a condition in which all experiences cease. There is no basis upon which to sense, to feel, or to will. The soul is in complete loneliness. Now the soul must find the presence of the spirit out of its own power. Without surrendering to passivity, it must find the strength for an impulse-to-action within itself. The soul's awakening at the moment of falling asleep—awakening itself through the strength of its own inner being, through the power of the I itself, without any motive for staying awake—is presence of the spirit (presence of mind). The soul is spiritually present when it is silent. The power of the soul to keep itself awake at the moment of falling asleep is this presence of spirit. It makes intuition possible, and is necessary for intuitional knowledge.

These first three trials—these first three experiences—represent the human ascent into the spiritual world. If we have here the threshold (see figure 6), then the ascent into the

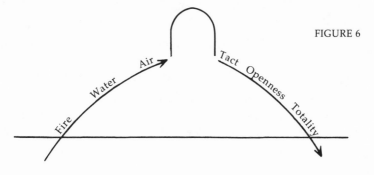

FIGURE 6

higher world occurs through these three stages, through these three trials. By means of them, one learns to ascend into the spiritual world and one finds the powers of courage, self-control, and spiritual presence. And by these, the experiences of imagination, inspiration, and intuition become possible.

If, having attained the necessary capacities, one ascends into the spiritual world, then the task arises within oneself to represent and demonstrate what one has seen, experienced, and endured there.

Then there begins the path of experience of such "representation." One enters into the *temple*; that is, one is admitted to the realization of the mysteries connected with the temple of humanity. We have already spoken about this temple—it is the same temple that Rudolf Steiner calls the Sun Temple in his *Mystery Dramas*. One enters the temple of the Sun. After one has passed through the Moon sphere in the trial by fire, the Mercury sphere in the trial by water, and the Venus sphere in the trial by air, one enters into the Sun sphere and thus into the Sun Temple.

The journey one makes on the path of spiritual discipleship is the same as the one that a person makes after death—namely, the path of the four stages.

The temple of the Sun is the ideal of future humanity. In this spiritual abode, into which one is admitted after the trial by air, one is met with a new experience. One must take an oath. Only if one takes the oath not to betray the secret of the temple—the ideal of the future—can one work toward its realization. Rudolf Steiner, in *Knowledge of Higher Worlds*, clearly expresses how this oath is to be understood. It is not a question of keeping something secret, but rather of learning to develop in oneself a new quality—the quality of spiritual tact. Consequently, we can also call this trial the "trial of tact." One learns what tact is—what is possible to say to different individuals. Only so much can be said as can be understood or encountered morally. The highest things can be revealed if they are united with a heartfelt note of morality. A mystery is "betrayed" if it is presented as mechanical, cerebral knowledge. Presented mechanically, cerebrally, it is something quite other than it ought to be.

The next thing that is necessary, in order to "represent" this temple into which one enters, is the experience called "the drinking of the draught of forgetfulness." Just as the oath was the trial of tact, so the so-called draught of forgetfulness is nothing other than a trial of openness, of freedom from prejudice. That is to say, this is a trial—or test—of trust in human beings. After having taken into oneself the higher knowledge of the temple, one must not despair at the difficulty of communicating this knowledge to others. Despite all the experiences to the contrary, one must realize that representing the truth is not hopeless. One must learn to trust human nature. The longing for truth, for the temple, lives in human nature. One must appeal to this longing. One must nurture the hope that it will shine through all the layers of disguise concealing it. Trusting in this, one must dare to represent these matters as one's tact directs.

The final test—expressed in acts and deeds—could be called the "trial of totality." This is a matter of drinking the draught of remembrance. That is, just as during the previous trial one had to learn to forget ordinary experiences—in order always to have present in one's consciousness the deeper experience of another person's higher I, and to have trust in humanity—so in this trial one must learn to maintain a continual capacity to remember all the knowledge and experiences that flow out of the spiritual world. Whereas in ordinary life one usually acts with a dim consciousness, one must now be in a state of awareness, acting with clarity of consciousness. To enable one to act with sunlit clarity, the spirit must become "instinctual." It must able to act with the sureness of instinct out of sunlit clarity, not out of reflection. This totality is the result of the presence in one's will of all that one has experienced. These are the fruits of all the insights and particular trials that lie on one's path. It is a matter of never forgetting experience—so that it might be continually present in one's will as well as in one's blood, and so that the corresponding insights might become transformed into deeds with lightning speed.

Thus we have a picture of the six trials, the six tests. Three lead into the spirit world and to the temple. Three involve the representation of the world of spirit in the physical world. If we return to the question which we raised earlier, the question of why the six exercises have such a fundamental significance for all pupils of the spirit, the answer is that each of the six exercises develops the particular inner strength that is needed later to successfully undergo the corresponding trial.

The entire path of initiation is contained in these six exercises. Thus, the power that flows into one's organization—developed through the control of thoughts—is the power that blossoms forth in the test of courage, in the trial by fire. And the power of endurance and inner self-command, which is developed through the control of action, proves itself in the trial by water. The control of feelings—the inner calm in the presence of joy and sorrow—is the strength that then proves necessary in the trial by air. Positivity, the recognizing of a positive element in every manifestation—tolerance, forbearance—is the faculty needed for the trial of tact towards others. Inner positivity makes tact possible in representing the temple in the world. The exercise of openness, of inner trust, creates the power which prepares the full development of the ability that is then experienced and developed in "drinking of the draught of forgetfulness" in the trial of openness. Finally, the sixth exercise, that of balance and of inner equanimity, transforms the five previous exercises into capabilities. Such inner equanimity is the ability to take in the draught of remembrance, whereby one is completely present and continually able to remember all the mysteries necessary for the fulfillment of the duties incumbent upon one.

We can see from this account what the essential principle of the exercises is. Leading, teaching personalities have always recognized the path humanity must tread and have summed it up in simple exercises. By means of these exercises one develops in advance the strength that will later prove itself in the corresponding trials of the path of spiritual discipleship, as well as in one's life experiences.

Again, the six exercises correspond to the six trials characterized by Rudolf Steiner in *Knowledge of Higher Worlds*. The six exercises are the preparation for these trials. In an elementary form, and on a smaller scale, the exercises are themselves the trials. The great trials come later. Thus the six exercises correspond to the six trials and also to the stages on the path of esoteric Christian initiation.

The first exercise, the control of thoughts, develops the current of a courage-like stream that is the same power we have already considered from several points of view—the power of the *washing of the feet*.

The power developed through the exercise of the control of actions is the power necessary for enduring the stage of the *scourging*, for passing through it. The scourging is the assault on a human being from the right and the left. Lucifer and Ahriman assail the human being simultaneously—yet one must find the strength not to follow them, but rather to follow the direction of the line that one has set oneself.

The third exercise, the control of feeling, is the inner expression of the power necessary to reach the stage of the *crowning with thorns.* Here it is a matter of being in command of one's feelings and, especially, of overcoming the feeling of pity—so that the duty arising out of love and the duty arising out of truth are not jeopardized.

Positivity, developed in the fourth exercise, will later make possible, by means of forbearance, the *carrying of the cross.* The exercise of positivity is the preparation for resolving to become one's brother's keeper. "Carrying the cross" describes the situation of the human soul that follows from the resolution to become "my brother's keeper." Only when one can perceive the positive element everywhere, when one has practiced positivity to such an extent that it has become an attribute of the soul, is it possible to bear the cross. Then one can bear the cross without complaint.

The fifth step, the exercise of openness and trust, is a preparation for the future stage of *crucifixion.* The crucifixion is the highest act of trust that one can possibly think of after one has endured, in a kind of Golgotha, the test of rigidity. If one finds the strength to place an equal degree of rigidity against the onslaughts of Lucifer and Ahriman—a rigidity composed of patience and waiting—then this is the highest level of trust toward humanity and toward karma that one can manifest.

The exercise of equanimity, or balance, prepares for the stage of the *entombment.* This continues the crucifixion and lies far off in the future. At the stage of entombment it is a question not only of motionlessly confronting the regions of death as a guardian of conscience, but of surrendering oneself to this realm of death. The exercise of equanimity is one of the fundamental principles of true occultism that a human being sows upon the fields of death. One becomes a sower in the regions of death. One does not expect immediate results but knows that what one creates goes through the realm of death. Equanimity, such as can be attained only at this stage, is necessary not to give up one's work, even though everything that one produces dies. The entombment is not only a power of imagination. It is also in a certain way inherent in human activity: one is consciously prepared to go on with what one must bring into the world, even though one knows that it will fall prey to death. One does this because one event—the resurrection—is still to come.

The greatest seriousness is at the same time the greatest responsibility, and the greatest responsibility occurs when a person, while working for the present, knows that everything will be dissolved by death and yet will rise again, will resurrect, because it is truth. This is equanimity. In its highest form, it reveals itself at the stage of entombment, but it has its preparation at the level of the exercise of equanimity.

The seventh stage of the Christian-Rosicrucian path is the *resurrection* which follows from the previous stages of crucifixion and entombment. Resurrection is not an exercise, but an event—a wonder awaiting humanity. This event is in the region of the Father, who through his lightning bolts and thunder presents revelations in both inner cognition and destiny. Resurrection is not attained through the practice of spiritual exercises; it is the answer that comes from the heavens. It comes to meet the efforts of one who ascends through the six stages of the Passion and goes through the six trials, or tests.

And so you see, dear friends, how profound is the legacy of Rudolf Steiner. The exercises are simply presented as elementary and basic—and yet how much lies hidden behind them and how far they lead when all the spiritual background is considered. In this sense, Rudolf Steiner was a "knower." The simple, clear, easily surveyable quality of what he gave had an enormous background in spiritual vision and experience.

We have spoken today about the path of this initiation from the point of view of practical exercises. Tomorrow we shall talk again about this path, but from a new perspective. We shall consider it from the point of view of the life-path of Rudolf Steiner; that is, from the perspective of one who during his life realized the stages of the Christian-Rosicrucian path that begins with the washing of the feet and ends with the entombment and the resurrection.

Rudolf Steiner's Life-Path
as the Way of the Christian Initiate

*D*EAR FRIENDS:

Yesterday we considered the exercises given by Rudolf Steiner, with their spiritual and moral background. Today, however, we shall not limit ourselves to seeking to understand the depths that lie behind what Rudolf Steiner taught; rather, we shall seek to understand the depths expressed in the life experiences Rudolf Steiner himself *lived*. We shall consider the course of Rudolf Steiner's life not as it appeared outwardly, but as it appears from within.

From within, Rudolf Steiner's life appears as a path leading through definite stages. These are the same stages, in fact, with which we have already been concerned. I should like to say, too, that it is extremely difficult to speak about the course of Rudolf Steiner's life. Because these events took place a relatively short time ago, one is compelled often and painfully to touch upon various matters that are still of "human" interest—for the lapse of time is insufficient to constitute the distancing that would make for an impersonal interest in the subject. Thus, in what I will have to say, it might appear that certain statements are intended as a reproach toward someone. I want you to know that nothing of this sort is intended. No criticism or reproach of anyone is meant. My only concern is to consider the course of

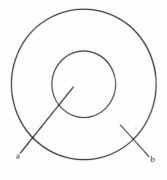

FIGURE 7

Rudolf Steiner's life in its moral-spiritual aspect.

It is a profound and remarkable fact that the childhood experiences of great personalities often foreshadow in abbreviated form what lies before them in the way of personal destiny. It is as if, unfolding in concentric circles, there comes to expression in a small circle what later appears in a larger circle. I can illustrate this with the help of a drawing (Figure 7). If you imagine the experience of childhood contained in *circle a*, you have a small picture of what later reappears in *circle b*. These concentric circles repeat themselves throughout life.

For this reason, as a way of insight into his life, we will consider briefly Rudolf Steiner's childhood. The keynote of this childhood is expressed by Steiner himself in his autobiography, *The Course of My Life*. In it, although he speaks of his parents, one can also see clearly how things were in relation to himself. Steiner writes of his father:

> My father was of the utmost good will, but of a temper—especially while he was still young—which could be passionately aroused. The work of a railway employee was to him a matter of duty; he had no love for it. While I was still a boy, he would sometimes have to remain on duty for three days and three nights continuously. Then he would be relieved for twenty-four hours. Thus life bore for him no bright colors; all was dull gray. He liked to keep up with political developments; in these he took the liveliest interest. My mother, since our worldly goods were not plentiful, had to

devote herself to household duties. Her days were filled with loving care of her children and of the little home.

In this you see the colors of Rudolf Steiner's childhood. The father, who experiences nothing colorful in life, only greyness; for whom the highest things in life are political questions; while the mother absorbs herself in housekeeping since no gifts of good fortune are present. Such was Rudolf Steiner's psychic and physical environment.

On the other hand, his surroundings were such that one side of life was filled with the railway and its traffic, the other side with nature. Thus, a little further on in his autobiography, he writes:

> It seems to me that passing my childhood in such an environment had a certain significance for my life. For my interest was strongly attracted by everything around me of a mechanical character. And I know that this interest tended constantly to overshadow in my childish soul the affection which went out to that charming and yet mighty nature into which the railway train, in spite of being in subjection to this mechanism, always disappeared in the distance.

Hence the existence of mechanical things in the life of this small child always tended to darken the life of the heart, which yearned for nature.

When Rudolf Steiner went to the village school, it happened that, because of an injustice, there was no place for him there. He was accused of doing something mischievous that he had not done. His father was indignant.

> My father was furious when I reported this matter at home. The next time the teacher and his wife came

to our house, he told them with the utmost bluntness that the friendship between us was ended, and declared, "My boy shall never set foot in your school again." Now my father himself took over the task of teaching me. And so I would sit beside him in his little office by the hour, and was supposed to read and write while he at the same time attended to the duties of his office.

So Rudolf Steiner was taken out of the school surroundings, away from other children, and had to learn to read and write in his father's office.

Then came another experience.

Once something happened at the station that was "shocking." A freight train rumbled up. My father stood looking toward it. One of the rear cars was on fire. The crew had not noticed this at all. The train arrived at our station in flames. All that occurred as a result of this made a deep impression on me. Fire had started in the car by reason of some highly inflammable material. For a long time I was absorbed in the question of how such a thing could occur. What those around me said to me about this was, as in many other cases, not to my satisfaction. I was filled with questions, and I had to carry these about with me unanswered. It was thus that I reached my eighth year.

In these first seven years of life which concluded with the fire on the railway train and the deep impression it made upon him, we have the first small concentric circle. We have the fact that Rudolf Steiner had to live in an environment, and in conditions, of material discomfort. The surroundings were grey and gifts of good fortune were not granted.

Rudolf Steiner's whole life was lived through under that sign.

Further, there was the fact of living between two worlds—of living between what was alive in the heart and what was symbolized by outer mechanistic culture and its corresponding human behavior. Heart on the one side; mechanical, material activity on the other.

The third note was struck by the event in the village school. There was no room for him in the culture of the time. Everywhere he was crowded out. He had to make room for himself—he was always a superfluous man in life. Every place was occupied. This began in his youth, when he had to leave school and learn in his father's office.

A prophetic foreshadowing of the future of his work was provided by the flames of the fire (which made such a deep impression upon him) and by the question that lived on in his soul: How is it possible that a fire can break out due to insignificant causes, and that a train can travel on in flames while people do not notice? When the Goetheanum went up in flames, it was the expression in the large circle of his life of what Rudolf Steiner experienced as a child in the railway station when the train was in flames. Thus the fundamental motifs of Rudolf Steiner's life were foreshadowed in these first events of his childhood.

Then, when Rudolf Steiner grew older and entered into the first friendships of his youth, the peculiar fact was that he participated very intensely in the interests of his friends, while what inwardly preoccupied him found no sympathy, no understanding. He writes in one place for example:

My youthful friendships in the time of which I am speaking had a peculiar relation to the course of my life. They forced me into a sort of double life of the soul. The struggle with the riddles of knowledge, which then filled my mind more than anything else, indeed always aroused in my friends a strong interest, but very little active participation. In the experience of these riddles, I remained rather lonely. On the other hand, I shared completely in whatever arose in the existence of my friends. Thus there flowed along in me two parallel currents of life: one that I followed like a lone wanderer, and one that I shared in vital companionship with persons bound to me by ties of affection. But the experiences of the second kind were also in many instances of profound and lasting significance in my development.

It was thus throughout his life. Rudolf Steiner took it upon himself to visit the most varied centers of thought and endeavor, but was himself visited by no one. He left the domain of his inner life, of his problems, of his own work in order to busy himself with the problems of others. Afterward, he returned to his alone-ness. This situation continued right through his life—including later on in the Theosophical Society and in the Anthroposophical Society. He always descended from the momentousness of his own struggles to enter into the circle of interests of other people. The different achievements of his life—anthroposophical medicine, eurythmy, speech formation, and so forth—came into being in this way. Thus Rudolf Steiner always left his own inner life in order to concern himself with the circle of interests of other people and to create what they needed.

This fundamental attitude of Rudolf Steiner's we may call the *washing of the feet*. Throughout his life, as his basic attitude, he fulfilled this gesture. From his earliest youth onward, he always inwardly bowed down and gave his attention to strivings and ideas that were on a lower level of development than that on which he himself lived. The greatest part of his energy and time was spent in giving such help on a lower level. This washing of the feet continued on throughout his entire life.

Rudolf Steiner adopted yet another attitude in his life, an attitude we can understand from the following incident described in *The Course of My Life*. Rudolf Steiner writes that when he was a student, he was chosen to be head of the students' assembly room.

> Later I was elected president of the Reading Hall. For me, however, this was a burdensome office, because I was confronted by the most diverse party viewpoints and I saw in all of these their relative justification. Yet the adherents of the various parties would come to me, and each would seek to convince me that his party alone was right. At the time when I was elected, every party had voted for me. For until then they had only heard that in the assemblies I had taken the part of what was justified. After I had been president for a half-year, all voted against me. They had then found that I could not decide as positively for any party as that party desired.

We could say that this is a simple case, but it points to something larger that runs throughout the course of his life—namely, Rudolf Steiner's position was always such that he stood, as it were, between two chairs. He had an inner attitude toward opposite human strivings, from which he could see and express what was relatively justified on either side. But when he had a decision to make, or when he was in a position where he could act, he always lost the position because he satisfied neither the one side nor the other.

Thus we can really say that Rudolf Steiner behaved in a neutral manner toward contending opposites. He behaved, that is, as one who had to represent the third element. It was this position of representing the third element that expressed itself—to give one example—when he had to give up the post of lecturer in a worker's school in Berlin, because he could not represent the Marxist system.

Similar events occurred within the Theosophical Society as well, and in the same way Rudolf Steiner was inwardly excluded from much that happened in the Anthroposophical Society. He was unable to bring many things to realization because he was often excluded from certain activities of the Anthroposophical Society. For his own activity there was no place. This was because, inwardly, he assumed the attitude of the *scourging*—for the attitude of the scourging is to stand between two opposing streams, being swayed neither to right nor to left, but holding oneself in the middle in spite of all attacks. A human being is so constituted physically that the left side is Luciferic, and the right side, Ahrimanic. In the body there is no place for the Christian element. The same is true of the whole of culture. It consists of Luciferic and Ahrimanic elements. Everything is taken up by these and no place is left in the world for the Christian element. A place for the Christian element must be constantly created and conquered and held against attacks that come from both sides.

Thus Rudolf Steiner stood in life as one who was constantly scourged, as one who had to endure attacks from religious, artistic, and scientific movements. He stood as one who had the power not only to have, but also to represent. He stood firm so that the third—the Christian—element might be represented in the world, where otherwise there is no place for it. We can say that for the whole of his life, from earliest youth to his last breath, Rudolf Steiner was exposed to this destiny. He had to stand between right and left, open to visible and invisible attacks. The streams that constitute life were always dissatisfied with the position he took. This is the inner spiritual attitude toward life which we can call Rudolf Steiner's scourging.

We can understand Rudolf Steiner's situation more deeply from the human point of view when we consider what it means for a person possessing open spiritual eyes and ears to stand in modern culture, surrounded by modern humanity. Inner seeing and inner hearing are extraordinarily delicate things and are accompanied by a refinement of the inner life. Coarse outer culture, the materialistic way of thinking, is something that, from the purely human standpoint, causes incessant blows to fall upon one who must repeatedly represent the spiritual that lives in the soul.

If we now inquire further into other aspects of Rudolf Steiner's life, we find that in the course of it there occurred a decisive spiritual event. This event occurred at about the end of the nineteenth century. Through it, Rudolf Steiner was decisively confronted with the whole picture of the actual situation of modern humanity. Confronted with sleeping humanity—for with regard to what was of decisive importance humanity was indeed asleep—he was faced with the task of deciding whether to present the truth in such a way that it would become both visible and audible for the consciousness of modern human beings. That is, Rudolf Steiner was faced with the decision of whether to create publicly a science of the spirit, to convey to humanity communications from the spiritual world. To be faced with this question really means much more than one may think, if one considers everything with regard to moral problems and other difficulties that arise when such a decision has to be consciously made.

Consider the situation. On the one hand, there is the picture of all the illusions in the world—for example, one sees before one's inner eye the great illusions of social movements. On the other hand, certain life experiences have made one quite aware that something spiritual, a purely spiritual teaching, can never be popular. All those who have already become involved with illusions are not going to retreat. The powers of resistance that are already present are enormous and will only be awakened the more when words bearing knowledge of the spiritual world are spoken.

Furthermore, one must consider that such a decision bears within it a certain overcoming of inner compassion. Such inner pity can be intense and can call forth the powerful inclination not to take people's illusions from them, because without their illusions people would begin to doubt what they still have. People are hurt and wounded when their illusions are taken away from them. It is a conscious act, therefore, when, in the service of truth, much pain is caused to other people. A certain "severity" (*Härte*) is required to make the decision to place the truth before those who have accustomed themselves to various illusions that support and comfort them.

There is a good deal more to Rudolf Steiner's decision to come forward, despite all this, with spiritual science. The hour when he became the representative of the spiritual world in the dark, materialistic world was the hour when he placed the crown of thorns on his head. Then he stood before the eyes of the world. Some looked upon him as a remarkable curiosity of the twentieth century. Others looked upon him as one who ought to be unmasked. A third group, however, looked upon him in such a way that they believed they.had received from him a final and complete revelation, one that made independent research and work superfluous. Instead of becoming anthroposophists, these became Steinerites.

Thus many eyes looked upon him, shamelessly seeking to disrobe him. Some were intent upon finding what was imperfect in him; others were intent upon following him blindly and passively. Thereby they set a seal on the future of his work and ensured that it would not be carried further. This *crowning with thorns*, which happened at the beginning of the twentieth century, lasted until the end of his life, as did the washing of the feet and the scourging.

In the movement, which was then known throughout the whole world as the Theosophical Movement, Rudolf Steiner found a group of dilettantish, but honest, people who were interested—superficially but honestly—in his work. He took upon himself the cross of taking charge of this community. He made the decision "to be his brother's keeper"—we have already spoken of the meaning of these words and do not need to dwell upon it further. I wanted only to say that he took charge of this community in which there lived much that was fruitless. He wanted to bring them far enough in their development that one day they would be capable of representing spiritual science. We must say that this *carrying of the cross*, which began when he linked himself to this group, was something that from the human point of view can appear quite differently than from a higher, birds-eye perspective. There developed in this community a certain ponderousness, a certain weight, which was consciously laid on him. It happened increasingly that people came forward who consciously, indeed willfully, laid their burdens upon Rudolf Steiner—not only their own personal burdens, but also those of the community. This found expression in the formula "The Doctor said..." This formula still lives on. With it, all independent striving has come to an end. A stop was put to all questioning and endeavor. Rudolf Steiner, who always said that it was a bad thing for authority to become decisive, became an authority in this community—not a great, impulse-giving, moral example, but an authority in the fruits of knowledge, in his words. Thus all his words were crucified, nailed down, with the formula, "The Doctor said..." That was something more painful to Rudolf Steiner than one might realize. He did not speak about it personally, only in general. What he had to bear, he alone knew. And one must say that for Rudolf

Steiner, for whom the spiritual work that he had to do in the world was the most important thing in life, this attitude was something that could give rise to hopelessness.

So it was that the World War broke out in 1914. Had the Anthroposophical Society risen to its tasks, this would not have happened. For representatives of all the karmic streams of humanity were present in the Anthroposophical Society, and there should have been peace between them. If the Society had then risen to the challenges placed before it through Rudolf Steiner, events would not have come to a world war. For this reason 1914 was a year of great despair for those who awaited from the Society the fulfillment of its mission.

In spite of all this, even during the World War, Rudolf Steiner continued to carry on with his work—though indeed under conditions quite different than before. During the war he was completely alone, and I mean alone not only in the human sense but also in the spiritual sense. For, in those times, Rudolf Steiner sacrificed the possibility of spiritual vision, of a clairvoyant connection with the spiritual world. During the period of the war he sacrificed, as it were, the last and highest thing that he possessed—his spiritual vision—and took upon himself the shattering spiritual task of being a representative of humanity with ordinary human consciousness. He did not want to be an exception. He wanted his karmic situation to be such that, during the events of the war, he would bring to expression a purely human knowledge and conscience. He wanted to demonstrate the worth of a purely human heroic deed and faithfulness to the spirit, so that this deed could then be placed upon the scales of the karma of all humanity.

During the World War, Rudolf Steiner was like a pillar, in the moral-spiritual sense of the word—a pillar connecting the spiritual world with the physical world not in clairvoyant vision, but in the wakefulness of the ordinary human faculties of conscience and faithfulness of will. It was a *presence*: there were moments when this presence was the *only* link that connected the Earth with the spiritual world.

There were moments, during the time of the war and after, when the Earth was connected with the heavens only by the thread of Rudolf Steiner's being. This was made possible through an awakened conscience. Rudolf Steiner stood as the embodied conscience of humanity. And one must say that, even during this time, it was not right in the eyes of everyone that he should stand thus—for the world was then divided into two parts who fought against each other. Rudolf Steiner was hated in Germany, even despised, as one who was unfaithful to his people. And abroad there were those (including anthroposophists) who turned away from him, regarding him as one who had fallen victim to German nationalism.

Thus it continued for a while. I can give you a shattering example. When Bolshevism broke out, there were quite a few anthroposophists living in Russia. Among them were a few leading personalities who were of the opinion that Bolshevism, despite its clumsy and distasteful forms, was the dawning of the sixth cultural epoch in Russia. Then a penciled note arrived in Moscow, a note that read: "Rudolf Steiner says that Lenin and Trotsky are enemies of humanity." Within twenty-four hours there was a revolution in the minds of the anthroposophists. This is something shattering—to realize how things actually were with regard to knowledge that should have stood essentially independently, and how, impelled by a mere note, there came about a change of mind that was superficial.

In this situation Rudolf Steiner was, I would say, the *awakener* of conscience. And you will all have noticed that a tragic tone increasingly pervaded his lectures from 1915 to 1918. He spoke more and more of the fact that humanity must awaken to what was urgently needed—but he continually knocked on closed doors. In spite of this, the Christmas Conference was inaugurated. All the inner powers that Rudolf Steiner had given up during the World War returned to him in an even finer and higher form.

During the Christmas Conference Rudolf Steiner took upon himself the task of becoming, externally speaking, President of the Anthroposophical Society—of which he had not previously been a member and which he previously led, so to speak, only from without. He became President, that is the external fact. Behind this fact stands the reality that Rudolf Steiner had made a deep karmic resolution to connect himself with this karmic community of human beings even more closely than before. By this deed he uttered the words that Christ Jesus once spoke to his disciples, namely, "I will remain with you always, even until the end of the Earth."

This is the inner meaning of the Christmas Conference: that Rudolf Steiner remains with the human stream, which he had formerly borne as a cross, and into which he now entered. That is the *crucifixion*.

People experienced the Christmas Conference as a happy event. Filled with joy, they reported the fact that Rudolf Steiner had again made it possible to set up a spiritual school, that he was now within the Society—as President. In reality, however, this was the crucifixion of Rudolf Steiner. This later manifested itself right into the physical realm. The illness which he developed, and which brought on his death, was such that he became motionless in his limbs—he could not walk.

Here I must speak of something of which I feel it is my human duty to speak. The fact that Rudolf Steiner could, to the very end, write and take a person's hand, is something we owe to a human being who stood by him lovingly, and who wrested the power of his hands from the illness. One woman achieved this. She was the person who stood faithfully by his side until the moment of death and prevented what was going to happen from coming about completely—that he would become completely motionless in all his limbs. The crucifixion was to have been complete. That it did not go as far as this, we owe to human help.

And then came the moment of his death. On the next day, lots were cast for his garments. People disputed over the honors he had left behind—what belonged to whom. This dispute over Rudolf Steiner's "garments" lasted a long time.

Then began a sequence of events (this was already after his death, but his life-path continues as an echo) in which people began to lay one portion after another of his work, piece by piece, into the grave. His ashes are preserved in an urn in the new Goetheanum. Many people go there every year. The building stands, and in it his lectures are repeatedly read aloud. But inwardly what is really happening is that Rudolf Steiner is being relegated more and more into the past. People speak of how he was, they quote what he said, they say what he authorized. All rights that are had and held go back to him. In both the cognitive and the practical life, the threads are traced back into the past. And at present Rudolf Steiner's being is becoming paler and paler. He is set back further and further into the past.

At such a time a human voice presuming to express something of his living being would be the most superfluous and damaging of voices. At present Rudolf Steiner is compelled to be silent. Everything fundamental has been said, there is no need to know more; his voice has become superfluous. What are necessary and significant, however, are the building, the books, the ashes in the urn, and the memory of the rights he conferred upon different individuals. He is the source of the rights that people now have. What is happening is the *entombment*. One could say that inwardly one hears—continually—the blows of the hammer, pounding shut the grave of Rudolf Steiner. Nails are constantly being hammered into the coffin in order that it should stay shut, so that Rudolf Steiner should not work on, his teaching not become clear, and people not meet him as a living being. Inwardly one hears the hammer blows on Rudolf Steiner's coffin, and these blows are the words of the formula: "The Doctor said..."—which means that he has already said everything. It means that he has spoken and therefore we need say nothing more. The hammer blows of death ring through the words, "The Doctor said..."

If we have this picture of the entombment inwardly before us, then we are compelled to face the question that our soul raises regarding the *resurrection*. At the present time we can hope for the resurrection of Rudolf Steiner: we can hope that people will give him the possibility of rising again, of being present, of doing deeds. Only if we do not limit ourselves to looking back upon the past, seeing in it the sole source of everything out of which it is possible to be creative, can we hope that this possibility will be given to Rudolf Steiner; only when monuments—not tombstones— are erected to him. Tombstones seal a grave, but a monument is a memorial, a pillar, a sign that enables people to enter into connection with the present. Thus there is hope, for if there are individuals inwardly prepared to stand in the sign of Rudolf Steiner's monument—to erect memorials to him in their inner being—then he will be able to fulfill what he intended when, during the Christmas Conference, he completed his deed of entering the Society as President. Then the possibility will be given to him of completing the deed he silently undertook to carry out—namely, "I will remain with you."

Rudolf Steiner was a follower and pupil of Christ Jesus. He portrayed him in the carved statue in the Goetheanum because he had met him. He walked the way of Christ Jesus, practicing the washing of the feet by becoming interested in others, while remaining alone in his own interests. Rudolf Steiner followed in the steps of the Master, in that he, Rudolf Steiner, was also a scourged one, crowned with thorns, who became his brother's keeper, went through all these stages on his life's journey, united himself with the karmic current of the Anthroposophical Society, and was crucified so that he could continue this path and "remain with you until the end."

Rudolf Steiner, as an entity, a being, has not ascended into higher spheres. He is here, he exists; and he knocks upon closed doors—closed because people look away, up to the hill, to the archives, saying, "The Doctor said..." Yet there is hope, for if we now turn our gaze to the spiritual world in our whole endeavor, if we again find in ourselves the courage to link ourselves *directly* with the world of spirit and to concern ourselves with it, if we turn our gaze to the spiritual world as the source of answers to our questions—then we can hope that a reunion with the living Rudolf Steiner will be possible. If we do not keep a living connection with the world of spirit, the doors will stay closed! But if, individually, we place ourselves in our inner moral consciousness in vertical alignment with the living spirit, there is hope that the seventh stage of Rudolf Steiner's life course, of his path-through-suffering, will find its realization. Indeed everyone, every anthroposophist, ought to become a human monument to Rudolf Steiner—to him whose presence is in the present.

It is not yet possible to speak of these things in a truly worthy manner, but I have spoken in such a way as has been possible for me to do at this time. I ask you once again to believe that I wish to criticize no one among those who belong to the Anthroposophical Movement, even if I seem to do so. I had only Rudolf Steiner in my mind's eye, and no one else.

REFERENCES
AND BACKGROUND READING

By Rudolf Steiner:

Knowledge of Higher Worlds and Its Attainment

Occult Science—An Outline

The Philosophy of Spiritual Activity

At the Gates of Spiritual Science

The Course of My Life

Karmic Relationships (Esoteric Studies), Volume III:
The Karmic Relationships of the Anthroposophical Movement

The Christmas Conference for the Foundation of the
General Anthroposophical Society 1923/1924

By Valentin Tomberg:

Anthroposophical Studies of the Old Testament

Anthroposophical Studies of the New Testament

For a free catalog
containing these and many other related titles,
write or call:

ANTHROPOSOPHIC PRESS
RR4, BOX 94 A-1
HUDSON, NEW YORK 12534
518-851-2054